# THE YEAR-ROUND BACKYARD BIRDS BOOK

## BIRDWATCHING GUIDE FOR BEGINNERS

BACKYARD BIRDING BOOK TO ATTRACT, IDENTIFY, & PHOTOGRAPH BIRDS OF NORTH AMERICA TO CREATE BIRD IDENTIFICATION RECORDS WITH DIY BIRDHOUSES, BIRD FEEDERS & BIRD SEED MIXES

DR. FANATOMY

# copyright@ dr. fanatomy 2024

All rights reserved. No part of this publication may be reproduced, distributed, or transmitted in any form or by any means, including photocopying, recording, or other electronic or mechanical methods, without the prior written permission of the publisher, except in the case of brief quotations embodied in critical reviews and certain other noncommercial uses permitted by copyright law.

This book is a work of non-fiction , and any resemblance to actual persons, living or dead, or actual events is purely coincidental.

The information and techniques described in this book are intended for educational and informational purposes only. The author and publisher shall not be held liable for any injury, damage, or loss arising from the use or misuse of the information presented in this book.

While every effort has been made to ensure the accuracy of the information contained within this book, the author and publisher make no warranties or representations, express or implied, about the completeness, accuracy, reliability, suitability, or availability with respect to the contents of this book for any purpose. The use of any information provided in this book is at the reader's own risk.

# TABLE OF CONTENTS

## 1. INTRODUCTION TO THE BACKYARD BIRDING (1-9)

- WHY BACKYARD BIRDING?
- BIRDING'S ENVIRONMENTAL IMPACT
- GETTING STARTED: ESSENTIAL BIRDING GEAR
- BIRD IDENTIFICATION
- BIRDING ETHICS: RESPONSIBLE OBSERVATION AND HABITAT PROTECTION
- TIPS TO BECOME A PROFICIENT BIRDER

## 2. ATTRACTING BIRDS TO YOUR BACKYARD (10-16)

- CREATING A BIRD-FRIENDLY HABITAT
- PROVIDING WATER SOURCES (BIRDBATHS & PONDS)
- CHOOSING THE RIGHT BIRDFEEDERS (TYPES & PLACEMENT)
- BIRDSEED MIXES: UNDERSTANDING BIRD DIETS
- USING SUET CAKES AND FEEDERS
- THE VITAL ROLE OF NATURAL FOOD SOURCES FOR BIRDS
- TABLE-COMMON BIRD SPECIES IN NORTH AMERICAN REGIONS - USA

## 3. IDENTIFYING COMMON NORTH AMERICAN BACKYARD BIRDS (17-48)

- AN INTRODUCTION TO BIRD ANATOMY AND TERMINOLOGY
- USING FIELD GUIDES AND BIRD APPS FOR IDENTIFICATION
- 20 COMMON BACKYARD BIRDS BY HABITAT

## 4. CREATING A BIRD IDENTIFICATION RECORD (49-55)

- KEEPING A BIRD JOURNAL: RECORDING YOUR OBSERVATIONS
- BIRD SKETCHING AND PHOTOGRAPHY TIPS
- BUILDING A LIFE LIST: TRACKING THE BIRDS YOU'VE SEEN
- REAL-TIME EXAMPLES: BIRD JOURNAL ENTRIES
- 20 MOST FAMOUS BACKYARD BIRDS: IDENTIFICATION GUIDE

# TABLE OF CONTENTS

## 5. DIY BIRDHOUSES, FEEDERS & SEED MIXES (56-78)

- BIRDHOUSES BASICS
- DIFFERENT TYPES OF BIRDHOUSES-10 TYPES
- BIRDHOUSE PLACEMENT AND MAINTENANCE
- SEASONAL MAINTENANCE TIPS
- COMPETITION: ENSURING ADEQUATE SPACE AND RESOURCES
- INTRODUCTION TO DIY BIRD FEEDERS
- TYPES OF FEEDERS FOR DIFFERENT SEED PREFERENCES
- DESIGNING SEED DISPERSAL MECHANISMS

## 6. BIRDING THROUGHOUT THE SEASONS (79-87)

- BIRD BEHAVIOR AND ACTIVITY IN SPRING & SUMMER
- BREEDING SEASON: NESTING AND CHICK REARING
- ATTRACTING BIRDS WITH NESTING MATERIALS
- FALL MIGRATION: WATCHING BIRDS ON THE MOVE
- WINTER BIRDING: PROVIDING FOOD AND SHELTER
- KEEPING WATER SOURCES ICE-FREE

## 7. SIZE, SHAPE, AND COLOR AS BIRDING TOOLS (88-98)

- UNDERSTANDING BIRD SIZE
- ANALYZING BIRD SHAPE
- WING AND TAIL SHAPE
- PATTERNS AND MARKINGS
- SEASONAL AND AGE-RELATED CHANGES
- COMBINING SIZE, SHAPE, AND COLOR FOR IDENTIFICATION
- BIRDING BY HABITAT
- SUMMARY AND PRACTICE
- PRACTICE EXERCISES

# TABLE OF CONTENTS

## 8. BEYOND YOUR BACKYARD: EXPLORING BIRDING LOCATIONS (99-107)

- FINDING LOCAL BIRDING HOTSPOTS
- NATIONWIDE SURVEYS
- REGIONAL MONITORING PROGRAMS
- ONLINE BIRDING FORUMS AND SOCIAL MEDIA GROUPS
- CREATING YOUR BIRDING LOGBOOK
- CONCLUSION

## 9. APPENDIX (108-121)

- APPENDIX 1 - GLOSSARY
- APPENDIX 2 - BIRD SEED MIX RECIPES FOR DIFFERENT SEASONS RESTORATION PROJECTS
- APPENDIX 3 - FREE ONLINE BIRD IDENTIFICATION RESOURCES
- APPENDIX 4 - SEASONAL BIRD MIGRATION CHARTS
- APPENDIX 5 - BIRD PHOTOGRAPHY TIPS
- APPENDIX 6 - BIRDWATCHING LOGBOOK PAGE

Welcome to the world of backyard birding! This chapter will explore how to attract birds to your space, the environmental benefits of birding, and the tools you need to get started.

**Why Backyard Birding?**

Birdwatching is an accessible and enriching hobby for people of all ages and abilities. It offers a glimpse into nature's delights.

- **Connect with Nature:** Take a step outside and submerge yourself in the natural world's vibrant and beautiful sights and sounds. Watch the brilliant colors of hummingbirds as they flit between flowers in the Southwestern part of the United States, enjoy the intricate songs of cardinals perched on branches in the Eastern US, or witness the captivating diving techniques of loons in a Canadian lake.

- **Relaxation and Stress Relief**: Research has shown that spending time in nature can reduce stress levels and promote feelings of well-being. Observing birds as they feed their young, construct intricate nests, or perform stunning aerial displays can be a calming and meditative experience.

- **Lifelong Learning**: The avian world is incredibly diverse, with over 10,000 known species. Backyard birding offers a continuous learning opportunity. You'll discover new bird species, learn about their unique behaviors and habitats, and constantly expand your knowledge of the natural world.

- **A Sense of Community**: Birding can be a solo activity, but it can also be an excellent opportunity to connect with like-minded individuals who share your passion for birds. You can join local birdwatching clubs, participate in citizen science projects that monitor bird populations, or engage with online birding communities to share your experiences and gain knowledge from other bird lovers across the continent.

Cardinal/ Redbird perched on a Twig

## TRIVIA FACTS-CARDINAL BIRD

- *Vibrant Plumage*: Male Cardinals boast striking red plumage, while females have subtler hues. Their appearance adds a vibrant touch to backyard settings.
- *Distinctive Song*: Cardinals' whistling songs are easily recognizable and often heard early in the morning and late at night, making them a familiar presence.
- *Year-round Residents*: These non-migratory birds are constantly in backyard feeders and gardens throughout North America.
- *Mated for Life*: Cardinals are monogamous and often seen in pairs. Both males and females participate in nest-building and raising their young.
- *State Bird*: The Northern Cardinal is the state bird for seven U.S. states, underscoring its cultural significance and popularity across the continent.

## Birding's Environmental Impact

Beyond the personal benefits, birding plays a crucial role in environmental conservation. Here's how:

- **Early Warning System**: Birds are important indicators of environmental well-being. By observing bird populations and their behavior, we can obtain valuable information about the health of our ecosystems. A reduction in bird populations in a specific area could indicate habitat loss, pollution, or the spread of disease.

- **Seed Dispersal**: Birds have an essential responsibility in the reproduction of plants. They help disperse seeds throughout their habitat by feeding on fruits and berries. This process assists plants in colonizing new areas and sustaining healthy ecosystems. For instance, the Pacific Northwest's lush forests and the Southwest's vibrant deserts are prime examples of regions that rely on birds to maintain the diversity of plant life.

- **Pest Control:** Many birds in backyards eat insects, which helps control pests that can damage gardens and crops. Eastern bluebirds, for example, are voracious insectivores and benefit farmers and gardeners across North America.

## Getting Started: Essential Birding Gear

Want to take your backyard birding experience to the next level? A few essential tools can make all the difference! And the best part? You don't need fancy or expensive equipment to get started.

- **Binoculars**: Your guide to observing birds up close: choose binoculars with 7x to 10x magnification and a wide field of view. Prioritize comfort while holding them.

- **Field Guides & Birding Apps**: Some resources can assist you if you want to recognize the feathered creatures inhabiting your backyard.

Field guides usually contain thorough illustrations and explanations of bird species native to your area. Birding applications offer similar capabilities, often with added features like bird songs and calls. Here are a few widely used options.

- **Field Guides**:
    - The National Audubon Society Field Guide to North American Birds (Eastern or Western Region)
    - Stokes Beginner's Guide to Birds

- **Birding Apps:**
    - Merlin Bird ID (by Cornell Lab of Ornithology)
    - Sibley's Birds (by David Allen Sibley)

- **Keeping a Bird Journal**: Tracking your backyard bird sightings is a great way to learn their behavior patterns and build a personal record of your adventures.

Here's an example entry for observing a North American bird:

| DATE & TIME | LOCATION | WEATHER CONDITIONS | SPECIES OBSERVED | DESCRIPTION OF THE BIRD | BEHAVIOR |
|---|---|---|---|---|---|
| April 5, 2024 | Backyard feeder | Sunny | American Robin | Medium-sized bird with a red breast and gray back | Feeding on worms in the lawn near the feeder |

American robin

By en:User:Mdf - Own work, CC BY-SA 3.0, https://commons.wikimedia.org/w/index.php?curid=253938

## TRIVIA FACTS- AMERICAN ROBIN

- **Unexpected Name Origin:** Did you know? The American Robin isn't actually related to its European namesake! Early settlers just thought they looked similar.
- **Flexible Flyers:** American Robins are champions of adaptation. Some populations migrate long distances for winter, while others stay put and form impressive social groups with hundreds, even thousands of birds!
- **Opportunistic Eaters:** American Robins are like feathered gourmands! They switch between yummy worms and juicy fruits throughout the year, even becoming occasional "drunk robins" when they indulge in fermented berries! (This is safe for them, don't worry!)
- **Busy Parents, Fierce Defenders:** American Robins are dedicated parents, raising multiple broods each season. Those bright orange bellies might be a signal to predators – "We're well-fed and ready to fight for our chicks!"
- **Symbol of Spring's Song:** More than just a pretty bird, the American Robin is a symbol of hope and renewal. Their cheerful song and arrival in spring mark the end of harsh winters and the promise of warmer days.

## Bird Identification

Identifying birds is a captivating pursuit that, while initially intimidating, becomes immensely rewarding with practice. Accomplished birders have a sharp eye and ear honed over years of observation. They approach bird identification as if unraveling a compelling mystery, piecing together hints from the bird's appearance, behavior, and surroundings. And what better place to commence this adventure than in one's backyard?

**Unveiling the Avian Puzzle**

Identifying birds involves considering various factors akin to assembling a puzzle. These factors include:

- **Shape and Size**: The physical characteristics of a bird, such as its size and posture, are pivotal in providing initial insights.

For instance, the sighting of a bird that is smaller than the commonly observed American Robin, yet possessing a distinctively cocked tail, is an excellent starting point for narrowing down the possibilities of the species. One can make an informed and accurate bird identification by paying close attention to these unique physical features.

- **Plumage and Field Marks:** When identifying a bird, note its plumage – feather patterns, colors, and markings. Specific field marks like brown feathers with chestnut hues and lighter undersides can help identify a bird. Use a field guide or app to match markings with illustrations or photos of bird species in your region.

- **Behavior:** Birds' actions and mannerisms help identify them. Watching them energetically hunt for insects on the ground and low branches while vocalizing and darting around can provide clues about their identity. Is it hopping or walking? Probing crevices or searching for seeds on the ground? These behaviors offer insights into their feeding habits and habitat preferences.

- **Habitat:** The bird's habitat preference can help narrow the list of potential species. Birds prefer specific habitats like open fields, dense forests, or urban environments.

- **Season:** The timing of the year can serve as an indispensable clue in identifying bird species, particularly during migration periods. Consider, for example, the occurrence of a particular bird in May in New Jersey. This may suggest a specific seasonal pattern, further facilitating its identification. Notably, while some bird species are permanent residents, others exhibit seasonal migration patterns. Familiarizing oneself with the typical seasonal occurrence of birds in the region can be an invaluable asset in identifying them.

- **Range:** Birds have different distributions, ranging from widespread to localized. Knowing a bird's usual range can help us identify it better.

Consider, for example, the occurrence of a particular bird in May in New Jersey. This may suggest a specific seasonal pattern, further facilitating its identification. Notably, while some bird species are permanent residents, others exhibit seasonal migration patterns. Familiarizing oneself with the typical seasonal occurrence of birds in the region can be an invaluable asset in identifying them.

- **Vocalizations**: Pay attention to bird vocalizations for clues to identify them. Familiarize yourself with familiar bird songs in your area using birding apps that offer audio recordings. Unique vocalizations, such as a chattering song resembling a sewing machine, can provide additional insight into a bird's identity.

## Birding Ethics: Responsible Observation and Habitat Protection

As you embark on your journey as a birdwatcher, being a responsible observer and protector of the environment is of utmost importance. To that end, it is essential to adhere to certain birding ethics designed to ensure birds' well-being and their habitats' conservation.

- Firstly, it is crucial to **minimize disturbance** while observing birds. Any loud noises or sudden movements could cause the birds to become frightened and abandon their nests, leaving their eggs or chicks vulnerable to predators. Therefore, speaking softly and moving slowly is advisable to avoid disrupting their natural behavior.

- Secondly, it is imperative to **respect nesting sites** and nesting birds. Nests are often well-hidden, so caution is recommended around areas where nesting activity is suspected. One should avoid approaching too closely or lingering for extended periods, as this could cause the birds to feel threatened or stressed.

- Thirdly, adhering to Leave **No Trace principles** when visiting birding locations is vital. You must pack out all trash, avoid disturbing vegetation, and respect any local rules or regulations.

- Fourthly, it is vital to **support habitat conservation** and protect bird populations. Supporting organizations that conserve bird habitats and natural areas is one way to achieve this goal. Another way is to create a bird-friendly haven in your backyard by planting native plants and providing feeders and birdbaths.

- Lastly, **reporting unusual sightings of birds** that seem out of place or injured to local wildlife authorities or bird observatories is highly recommended. This information can be valuable for tracking bird populations and migration patterns.

By following these birding ethics, you can ensure that your enjoyment of birds goes hand-in-hand with their well-being and the conservation of their habitats. Remember, responsible birding benefits both the birds and the future of birdwatching for generations to come.

**Tips to Become a Proficient Birder**

To identify birds, use these tips:

- Observe everything, including appearance, behavior, and habitat.
- Use resources like field guides, apps, and online resources.
- Keep a bird journal to track progress and learn patterns.
- Connect with birdwatching communities.
- Practice listening to bird songs.
- Be patient and persistent.

With dedication, you can become a proficient birder and discover the fascinating world of birds in your own backyard!

# Chapter 2: Attracting Birds to Your Backyard

Welcome back to the beautiful world of backyard birding!

This chapter will explore the exciting world of creating a bird-friendly sanctuary in your backyard. By providing the essentials - food, water, and shelter - you can transform your outdoor space into a bustling hub of avian activity, offering endless entertainment and ecological benefits.

## Creating a Bird-Friendly Habitat

Imagine your backyard transformed into a welcoming oasis for birds.

Here's how to achieve this:

### Selecting Native Plants and Trees:

- Native plants and trees offer a multitude of benefits:

  - **Food Source**: They provide natural food sources for birds, including fruits, berries, nuts, and insects attracted to the foliage.
  - **Shelter**: Dense foliage offers nesting sites and protection from predators.
  - **Sustainability**: Native plants are adapted to your local climate, requiring less maintenance and water.

- Examples of bird-friendly native plants:

  - **Shrubs**: Lilacs, viburnums, dogwoods, serviceberries
  - **Trees**: Oaks, maples, pines, birches
  - **Flowers**: Coneflowers, sunflowers, black-eyed susans, columbine

## **Providing Water Sources (Birdbaths & Ponds):**

- Fresh, clean water is essential for birds, especially during hot weather. Birds use water for drinking, bathing, and preening their feathers.

- **Birdbaths:**
    - Choose a birdbath with a shallow depth (1-3 inches) ideal for birds to bathe comfortably.
    - Place the birdbath in a shaded area away from predators but with a clear view so birds can easily spot it.
    - Keep the water clean and fresh, refreshing it every few days, especially during hot weather.

- **Ponds:**
    - Ponds offer a more significant water source that can attract a wider variety of birds.
    - Consider installing a small pond with gently sloping edges for easy bird access.
    - Ponds require more maintenance than birdbaths but can become a beautiful focal point in your backyard.

## **Choosing the Right Birdfeeders (Types & Placement):**

Bird feeders provide a supplemental food source, especially during winter when natural food sources are scarce.

**Types of Bird Feeders:**

Tube feeders: Ideal for offering seeds like black oil sunflower seeds, mixed seed blends, or Nyjer seeds for finches.

- **Hopper feeders**: Great for offering larger seeds like shelled peanuts or corn kernels.

- **Platform feeders** are suitable for offering a variety of foods, such as fruits, mealworms, suet cakes, or even peanut butter-smeared bread crumbs.

- **Hummingbird feeders**: Designed with specialized ports for hummingbirds to access sugar water.

## Placement:

- Hang feeders 5-6 feet away from windows, walls, or fences to prevent birds from colliding.
- Place feeders in open areas with some nearby cover where birds can quickly retreat from predators.
- Space feeders out to avoid overcrowding and competition between birds.
- Clean your feeders regularly to prevent the spread of diseases.

| FEEDER TYPE | SUITABLE SEED MIXES | COMMON BIRDS ATTRACTED |
|---|---|---|
| Tube Feeder | Black oil sunflower seeds, mixed seed blends, nyjer seeds | Finches, chickadees, nuthatches, goldfinches |
| Hopper Feeder | Shelled peanuts, corn kernels | Cardinals, jays, crows, grackles |
| Platform Feeder | Fruits (sliced apples, oranges), mealworms, suet cakes, peanut butter mix | Robins, woodpeckers, blue jays, thrashers |
| Hummingbird Feeder | Sugar water (1 part sugar to 4 parts water) | Hummingbirds |

# Birdseed Mixes: Understanding Bird Diets

Birds have diverse dietary needs. Offering various food options will attract a broader range of feathered visitors.

## Seed Preferences of Common Backyard Birds:

- **Finches**: Black oil sunflower seeds, nyjer seeds, thistle seed mixes.

- **Chickadees & Nuthatches**: Black oil sunflower seeds, mixed seed blends with suet pieces and peanuts.

- **Cardinals & Jays**: Mixed seed blends with larger seeds like sunflower seeds, cracked corn, and peanuts.

- **Hummingbirds**: Sugar water solution (1 part sugar to 4 parts water).

## Making Your Seed Mixes:

You can create your own customized seed mixes to attract specific bird species. Here are some tips:

- **Research**: Identify the birds commonly found in your area and learn about their preferred food sources.

- **Ingredients:** Choose high-quality seeds like black oil sunflower seeds, nyjer seeds, millet, cracked corn, and peanuts in varying proportions based on the birds you want to attract.

- **Freshness:** Use fresh seeds and avoid mold or mildew. To maintain freshness, store leftover seeds in airtight containers in a cool, dry place.

- **Cost-Effectiveness:** Making your mixes can be more cost-effective than buying pre-made blends.

**Using Suet Cakes and Feeders:**

- **Suet** is a high-energy food source made from rendered beef fat. It's a valuable winter food source for insect-eating birds like woodpeckers, chickadees, nuthatches, and wrens.

- **Suet Feeders**: Suet cakes are typically placed in wire mesh suet feeders to deter larger animals while allowing birds to access the suet.

- **Alternatives**: Consider offering peanut butter suet cakes made with vegetable shortening instead of beef fat for a vegetarian alternative.

## The Vital Role of Natural Food Sources for Birds

Encouraging birds to eat natural food sources in your backyard is essential for their health, even if you use feeders to attract them.

**Planting Fruit & Berry Bushes:**

Planting native fruit and berry bushes provides birds with a natural and sustainable food source. Some excellent choices include:

- Berries: Blueberries, raspberries, elderberries, hollies
- Fruits: Crabapples, cherries, dogwoods

**Encouraging Insects (Beneficial for Chicks):**

Insects are a crucial food source, especially for young birds. Here are ways to encourage a healthy insect population:

- **Minimize pesticide use**: It's important to note that pesticides kill harmful insects and beneficial ones that birds rely on for food. Opt for natural pest control methods to maintain a healthy bird food chain whenever possible.

- **Create a brush pile**: A brush pile made from branches and leaves provides shelter for insects and other small creatures that birds love to eat.

- **Let some flowers go to seed**: Native flowering plants attract pollinators like butterflies and bees, attracting insect-eating birds.

## Common Bird Species in North American Regions - USA

| REGION | STATES | KEY FEATURES | COMMON BIRD SPECIES | ATTRACTING BIRDS WITH NATIVE PLANTS |
|---|---|---|---|---|
| Northeast | ME, NH, VT, MA, RI, CT, NY, NJ, PA | Appalachian Mountains, New England coastline | Eastern Bluebird, American Robin, Northern Cardinal, Common Yellowthroat, Cedar Waxwing | Berry-producing shrubs like winterberry and viburnum, seed-bearing plants like sunflowers and coneflowers, insect-attracting flowers like columbine and goldenrod |
| Mid-Atlantic | DE, MD, DC, VA, WV | Chesapeake Bay, Blue Ridge Mountains | Carolina Chickadee, Tufted Titmouse, Northern Mockingbird, Baltimore Oriole, Eastern Towhee | Native plants like dogwood trees with delicious fruits, Virginia creeper for nesting, butterfly milkweed to attract insects |
| Southeast | KY, TN, NC, SC, GA, FL, AL, MS, LA | Gulf Coast, Appalachian Mountains | Great Kiskadee, Northern Mockingbird, Brown Thrasher, Yellow-rumped Warbler, Indigo Bunting | Nectar-rich flowers like hibiscus and trumpet honeysuckle, fruiting shrubs like southern magnolia and beautyberry |
| Midwest (Great Lakes) | OH, MI, IN, IL, WI, MN | Great Lakes, Mississippi River | American Goldfinch, Song Sparrow, Common Grackle, Eastern Phoebe, Northern Flicker | Seeds from native plants like coneflowers and black-eyed susans, berries from serviceberry bushes, winter food sources like crabapple trees |
| Southwest | TX, OK, AR, NM | Gulf of Mexico coastline, deserts | Curve-billed Thrasher, Lesser Goldfinch, Northern Cardinal, Bewick's Wren, Greater Roadrunner | Xeriscaping with drought-resistant plants like cacti with edible flowers, desert willow, and ocotillo |
| Rocky Mountains | CO, WY, MT, ID, UT | Rocky Mountains, Great Basin | American Robin, Steller's Jay, Dark-eyed Junco, Western Tanager, Mountain Chickadee | Fruits, seeds, and insects from plants suitable for higher altitudes like serviceberry trees, Gambel oak, and flowering currant |
| West Coast | CA, OR, WA | Pacific coastline, Sierra Nevada Mountains | Anna's Hummingbird, Spotted Towhee, California Scrub-Jay, Western Meadowlark, American Robin | Nectar-rich flowers like fuchsia and hummingbird honeysuckle, coastal plants like California lilac and coyote bush |

# Common Bird Species in North American Regions - Canada

| REGION | PROVINCES | KEY FEATURES | COMMON BIRD SPECIES | ATTRACTING BIRDS WITH NATIVE PLANTS |
|---|---|---|---|---|
| Atlantic Canada | NL, PE, NS, NB | Atlantic coastline, rugged terrain | Common Loon, Black-capped Chickadee, Song Sparrow, American Goldfinch, Northern Gannet | Nesting cover with spruce trees, berry-producing shrubs like wild raspberry and elderberry. Consider installing nesting platforms or boxes for seabirds. |
| Central Canada | QC, ON | St. Lawrence River, Great Lakes, Canadian Shield | Blue Jay, American Robin, Common Grackle, Ruby-throated Hummingbird, Cedar Waxwing | Maple trees for seeds, flowering shrubs like lilacs and viburnums for nectar, mountain ash trees with berries for robins and waxwings. |
| Prairie Provinces | MB, SK, AB | Prairie landscapes, agriculture | Northern Flicker, American Goldfinch, Song Sparrow, Red-winged Blackbird, Western Meadowlark | Native wildflowers like asters and goldenrod for insects, shrubs like chokecherry and saskatoon for fruits, spruce trees for winter cover. |
| British Columbia | BC | Pacific coastline, Rocky Mountains, rainforests | Varied Thrush, Stellar's Jay, Anna's Hummingbird, American Robin, Rufous Hummingbird | Salmonberry shrubs for fruit, red flowering currant for hummingbirds in coastal areas. Pines and crabapple trees in mountainous regions. |
| Northern Canada | YT, NT, NU | Arctic landscapes, tundra, wilderness areas | Snowy Owl (winters), Common Raven, Rock Ptarmigan, Snow Bunting, White-winged Dove (rare visitor) | Dead snags for cavity-nesting birds like owls. Research local regulations regarding attracting wildlife. |

# Chapter 3: Identifying Common North American Backyard Birds

Welcome back, my fellow birding enthusiasts!

Now that you've transformed your backyard into a haven for feathered friends, it's time to delve into the exciting world of bird identification. This chapter will equip you with the tools and knowledge to recognize and identify the feathered visitors gracing your backyard.

## An Introduction to Bird Anatomy and Terminology

**Bird Anatomy**: Familiarizing with basic bird anatomy will help you understand the terminology used in field guides and bird apps. Here are some key features:

- **Bill**: Bill shapes vary depending on the bird's diet. Thick bills are used for seed-eaters, and long and pointed bills are used for insectivores. The bills are used for feeding, grooming, and manipulating objects.

- **Wings:** Songbirds have short, rounded wings for maneuvering, while hawks have broad wings for soaring.

- **Tail:** During flight, the tail plays a crucial role in maintaining balance and steering. The length and shape of the tail can be used to identify specific species.

- **Legs and Feet:** Different types of birds have adapted leg length and foot structure for their lifestyles. For example, perching birds have three toes pointing forward and one backward for grasping branches, wading birds have long legs for navigating water, and swimming birds have webbed feet for propulsion.

- **Plumage:** Feathers serve as insulation, camouflage, and waterproofing. Observe color patterns, markings, and sex differences.

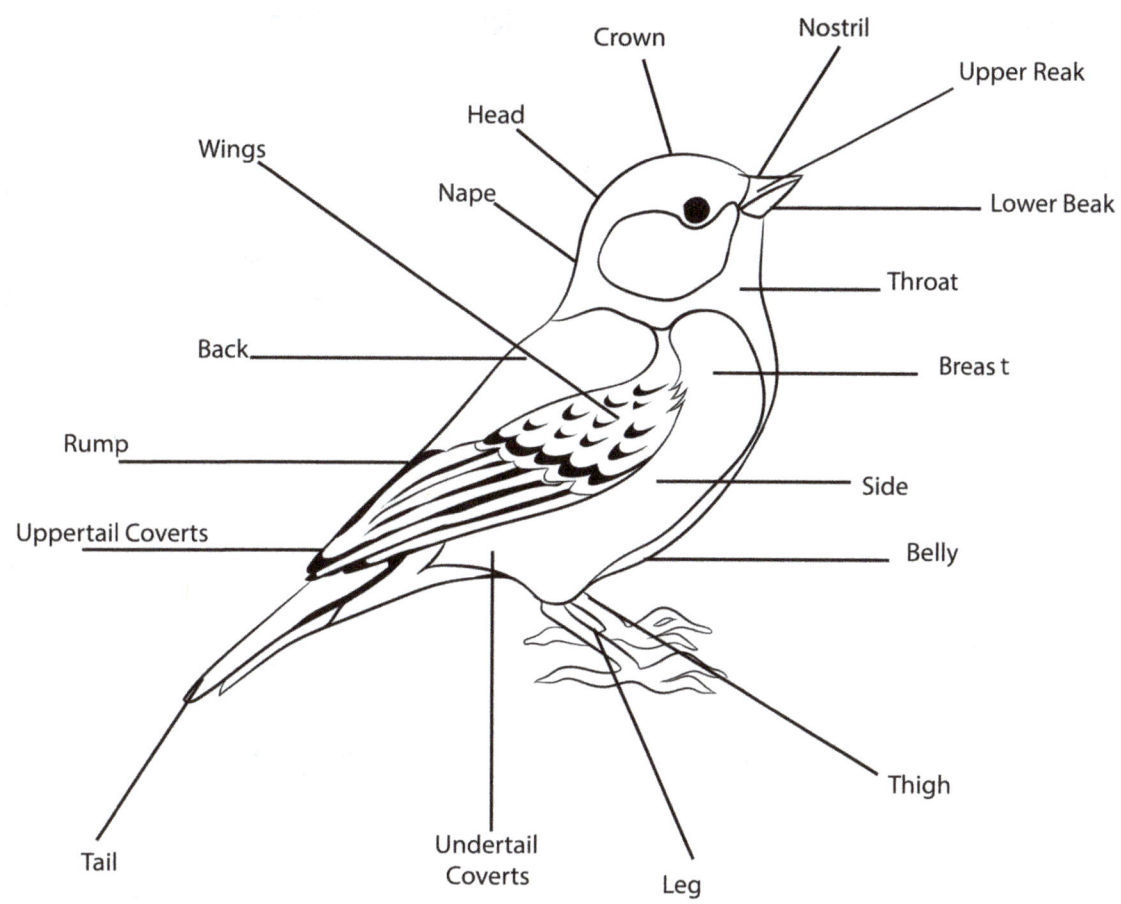

Bird- External Body Parts

**Bird Terminology**: Field guides and apps often use specific terms to describe bird features. Here are some common ones:

- **Crown**: Top of the head.
- **Nape**: Back of the neck.
- **Lores**: Area between the bill and the eye.
- **Rump**: Area between the back and the tail.
- **Flanks**: Sides of the body below the wings.
- **Breast**: Underside of the body between the neck and belly.
- **Barring**: Horizontal stripes on feathers.
- **Streaking**: Vertical stripes on feathers.
- **Patch**: Solid area of color on the plumage.

## Using Field Guides and Bird Apps for Identification

**Field Guides**: Birders consider field guides essential tools. These guides include detailed descriptions and illustrations of bird species found in your region. Pick a field guide specific to your location to make the best choice. Look for guides with high-quality illustrations or photographs that highlight key identification features. You can use the field guide's index and keys to narrow your search based on size, shape, color patterns, and habitat.

**Bird Apps**: Many smartphone apps can assist with bird identification. Here's how to leverage them:

- Use the app's photo identification feature by uploading a picture of the bird you observed.
- Some apps allow you to record bird songs and calls, which can be helpful for identification.
- Many apps offer interactive range maps and habitat information for bird species.

| APP | ACCESSIBILITY | COVERAGE | TOOLS | INTERFACE | COMMUNITY |
|---|---|---|---|---|---|
| Merlin Bird ID | Offline/Online | Extensive | Image Recognition, Sounds, Behavior | User-friendly | Engaging Platform |
| Audubon Bird Guide | Mostly Offline | Wide Range | Image Recognition, Sounds, Insights | Clean & Intuitive | Limited |
| eBird by Cornell | Mostly Online | Global | Sighting Reports, Maps, Hotspots | User-friendly | Strong Engagement |
| iBird Pro Guide | Mostly Offline | Comprehensive | Image, Sound, Profiles, Insights | Intuitive & Detailed | Limited |
| BirdNET | Online | Sound Focused | Sound Recognition | Simplistic & Visual | Limited |

# Key Features to Look For in Bird Identification & My Take

| FEATURE | DESCRIPTION | EXAMPLE |
| --- | --- | --- |
| Size | Overall size of the bird compared to a familiar reference point (e.g., robin, sparrow) | A hawk is larger than a robin, while a chickadee is smaller. |
| Shape | General body shape (e.g., plump, slender, long-necked) | A robin has a plump body, while a woodpecker has a long, slender body. |
| Coloration | Plumage color patterns, markings, and variations between genders | A male Northern Cardinal is bright red, while the female is reddish-brown. |
| Behavior | How the bird moves, feeds, and interacts with its environment | A woodpecker hammers on trees with its bill, while a hummingbird hovers while feeding on nectar. |
| Song & Calls | Unique vocalizations of the bird | A robin sings a clear, cheerio song, while a blue jay has a loud, harsh call. |

| PARAMETER | BEST APP |
| --- | --- |
| Image Recognition | Merlin Bird ID |
| Sound Recognition | Merlin Bird ID |
| User-friendly Interface | Merlin Bird ID |
| Community Engagement | eBird by Cornell |
| Comprehensive Coverage | iBird Pro Guide |
| Offline Access | Merlin Bird ID |
| Sound Focused Identification | BirdNET |
| Online Access | eBird by Cornell |
| Free Use | Merlin Bird ID, eBird by Cornell, iNaturalist |
| In-app Purchases | Sibley Birds |

# 20 Common Backyard Birds by Habitat

Prepare to meet some of the possible birds living in your area! This section showcases common backyard birds found in North America, classified by their preferred habitat. It is important to note that these are just examples, and the birds you observe may differ depending on your specific location.

Let's meet the common backyard birds of North America:

## (1) Northern Cardinal (Cardinalis cardinalis):

- **Range**: Eastern North America, from southern Canada to Mexico.
- **Description**: A vibrant red bird with a prominent crest (male), red-brown with olive accents (female). Feeds on seeds, fruits, and insects.

Northern Cardinal

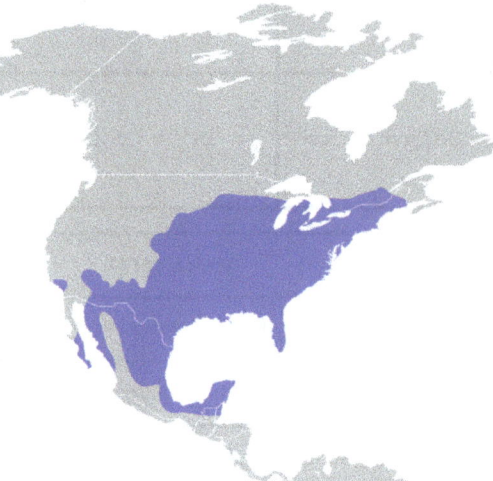

Northern Cardinal Year Round Range

Attribute: By Jebbles – This file was derived from BlankMap-World.svg;, CC0, https://commons.wikimedia.org/w/index.php?curid=108089052

**Diet** : The Northern Cardinal is an omnivorous ground-foraging bird that eats a wide variety of foods, including seeds, fruits, insects, grains, and nuts.

**Backyard Tips:**

To attract Northern Cardinals to your backyard:

- Provide shelter: Plant trees and bushes at different heights for privacy. In winter, cardinals prefer coniferous trees.

- Offer a feeder: Cardinals prefer feeders with large perches for large seeds like sunflower, safflower, and white milo seeds.

- Plant berries: Cardinals love dogwood berries.

- Avoid reflective surfaces: Remove reflections from windows or mirrors near feeding and nesting areas.

### (2) American Goldfinch (Spinus tristis):

- **Range:** Breeds across most of North America, winters in the southern US and Mexico.

- **Description:** Small, bright yellow bird with black wings. It feeds on seeds and thistles.

- **Diet** : American goldfinches mainly eat seeds from composite plants, grasses, and trees. They also consume insects and other plant matter, including buds, bark, and maple sap. Insects are eaten in small amounts during summer, and invertebrates are fed to their young in spring and summer.

Male American Goldfinch in summer plumage

By Rodney Campbell - GoldfinchUploaded by snowmanradio, CC BY 2.0, https://commons.wikimedia.org/w/index.php?curid=20388809

Female American Goldfinch

By Darren Swim - Own work, CC BY-SA 3.0, https://commons.wikimedia.org/w/index.php?curid=7859712

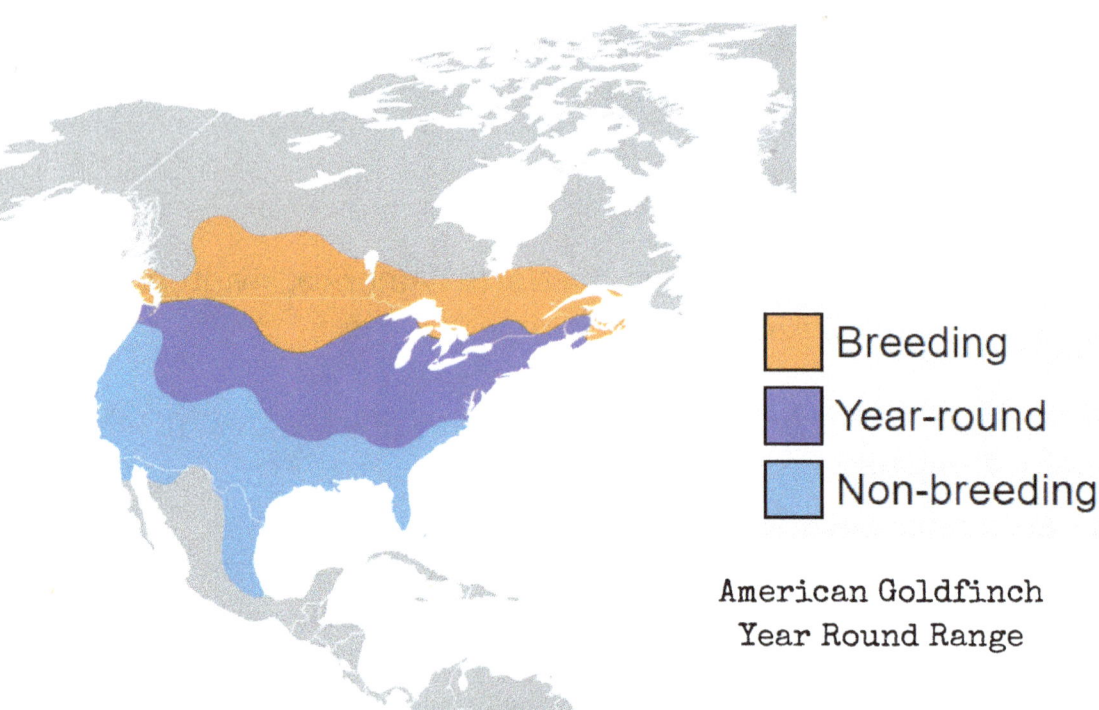

American Goldfinch Year Round Range

By Jebbles - This file was derived from: BlankMap-World.svg:, CC0, https://commons.wikimedia.org/w/index.php?curid=108088904

**Backyard Tips:**

Tips for attracting American goldfinches to your backyard:

- Provide sunflower and Nyjer seeds.
- Choose a feeder that allows climbing and hanging.
- Clean feeders once a month.
- Plant native thistles, milkweed, sunflowers, and other composite plants.

### (3) Black-capped Chickadee (Poecile atricapillus) :

- **Range:** Found throughout most of North America (from northern United States to southern Canada and up to Alaska and Yukon)

- **Description:** Small, plump bird with a black cap, white cheeks, and a gray back.

- **Diet:** Feeds on insects, seeds, and nuts.

Carolina chickadee

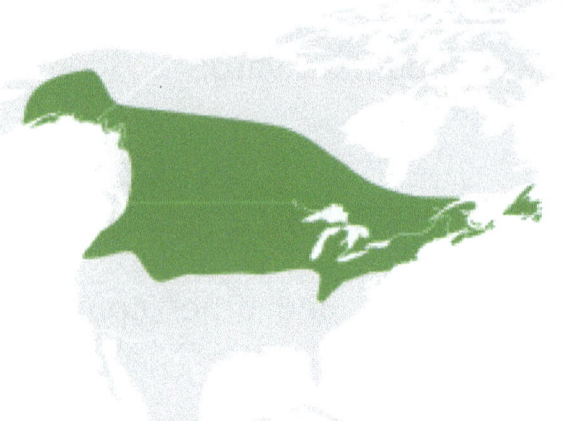

Range of Black-capped Chickadee

By Haller1962 - Own work, CC BY-SA 4.0, https://commons.wikimedia.org/w/index.php?curid=46922520

- **Backyard Tips:** If you want to attract Black-capped Chickadees (Poecile atricapillus) to your backyard, here are some tips you can follow:

- Offer food: Chickadees like peanuts, sunflower seeds, and suet. To attract them, you can use windows or tiny hanging feeders that swing in the wind.

- Provide nesting boxes: Install nesting boxes in undisturbed areas of your yard. Black-capped Chickadees usually nest in cavities in dead trees, rotting logs, or woodpecker cavities. They also use nest boxes when provided and line the nest with moss, animal fur, or other soft fibers.

- Plant trees: You can attract chickadees by planting willow, alder, and birch trees, which provide nesting habitats.

- Offer water: Chickadees visit birdbaths for drinking and bathing. You can provide a shallow birdbath with river rocks or gravel for perching. Drippers can also attract them because they like moving water.

- Listen for calls: Chickadees are often heard before they're seen and are attracted to birders making pishing sounds. Once you've learned their calls, you can listen for them and look for the flocks they travel in.

## (4) House Wren (Troglodytes aedon):

- **Range:** It is found throughout most of the Americas, from southern Canada to southern South America, making it the most widely distributed bird in the Americas.

- **Description:** Small, brownish bird with a relatively plump body shape. Rather than a cocked tail, they hold their tail erect most of the time. They lack a white eyebrow stripe, a helpful distinction from other wren species.

- **Diet:** Primarily insectivores, feeding on a variety of insects and spiders

House Wren
By S. King, US NPS – [1] at US NPS, Public Domain, https://commons.wikimedia.org/w/index.php?curid=8156486

Range of House Wren

By Cephas – BirdLife International. 2017. Troglodytes aedon (amended version of 2016 assessment). The IUCN Red List of Threatened Species 2017: e.T103886826A111242743. https://dx.doi.org/10.2305/IUCN.UK.2017-1.RLTS.T103886826A111242743.en. Downloaded on 19 May 2018., CC BY-SA 4.0, https://commons.wikimedia.org/w/index.php?curid=69286213

**Backyard Tips**

- Wrens are birds that prefer brush piles as cover, protection, and a place to find insects. If you plan to prune trees or cut brush in your yard, you can create a brush pile that can serve as a safe gathering place for birds.

- Additionally, you can hang a nest box to attract a breeding pair of birds.

- Installing the nest box well before the breeding season begins is important.

- You can also attach a guard to protect the eggs and young birds from predators.

**(5) Song Sparrow (Melospiza melodia) :**

- **Range:** Found throughout most of North America. They are year-round residents in some areas, but many populations migrate south for the winter.

- **Description:** A talented singer, the song sparrow can often be heard scratching amongst the leaves on the ground. Look for them near bushes and hedges. Their straightforward, whistled song is a familiar melody in many backyards.

- **Diet:** They like to forage for insects and seeds.

- **Backyard Tips:** To attract song sparrows, plant blackberries, blueberries, mulberries, pokeberries, and bayberries, as well as buckwheat, ragweed, clover, sunflower, wheat, rice, strawberries, raspberries, and wild cherries. Provide shelter by putting up a nest box and leaving leaves or raking them under plantings in winter. Install a birdbath or shallow water dish for drinking and bathing.

Song Sparrow

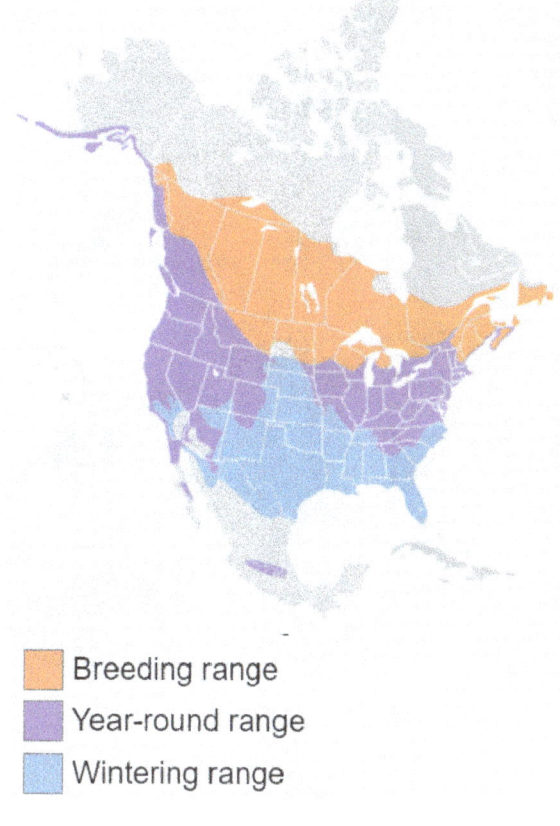

Range of Song Sparrow

By Cephas – Adpated from : Song Sparrow, Peter Arcese, Mark K. Sogge, Amy B. Marr, and Michael A. Patten. Birds of The World, The Cornell Lab of Ornithology. https://birdsoftheworld.org, CC BY-SA 4.0, https://commons.wikimedia.org/w/index.php?curid=107721151

## (6) American Robin  (Melospiza melodia) :

- **Habitat:** Found throughout most of North America (except Hawaii, northern Alaska, and northern Canada) in open woodlands, fields, and backyards. They migrate south in winter, reaching Mexico and Guatemala.

- **Description:** Large songbirds (7.9-11 inches long) with gray-brown bodies, orange breasts, and dark heads. Males have black streaks on their throats and rusty bellies, while females have paler heads.

- **Diet:** Mainly earthworms, insects, and fruits. They forage on the ground in spring and summer, switching to fruits and berries in winter.

American Robin

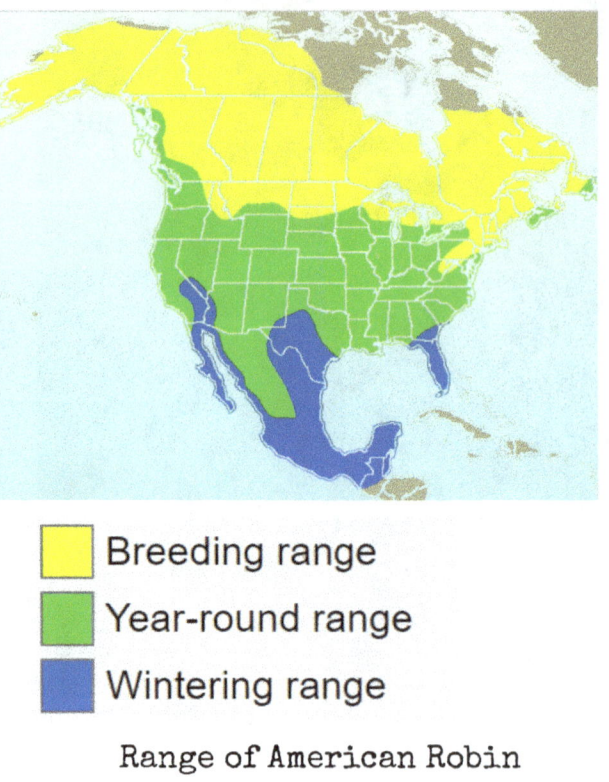
Range of American Robin

By Ken Thomas - http://www.kenthomas.us (personal website of author), Public Domain, https://commons.wikimedia.org/w/index.php?curid=34744124

**Backyard Tips:**

- Offer nesting boxes before breeding season.
- Place feeders with mealworms, suet, and fruits.
- Observe flocks in trees and near fruiting trees in winter.
- Avoid pesticides to attract insects for robins to eat.

**(7) House Finch (Haemorhous mexicanus):**

- **Range:** House Finches are prevalent across most of North America, excluding the far north. While many populations are year-round residents, some migrate southward during winter.

- **Description:** House Finches, with their vibrant red-breasted plumage, are a delightful sight at backyard feeders. These agile birds entertain observers with acrobatic feats, effortlessly clinging to feeders in various positions while indulging in seeds. Their cheerful, high-pitched, warbling song adds a delightful melody to the backyard soundscape.

House Finch

Range of House Finch

By Cephas - Own work, CC BY-SA 3.0, https://commons.wikimedia.org/w/index.php?curid=7872947

**Diet:** House finches (Haemorhous mexicanus) eat a variety of foods, including seeds, buds, flowers, leaves, and fruits year-round.

**Backyard Tips:**

If you want to attract House Finches to your backyard, here are some tips that might help:

- Offer their favorite foods: Fill the feeders with small, black-oil sunflower seeds, Nyjer, mixed birdseed, peanuts, fruit, suet, and sugar water.

- Provide a bird bath: A bird bath that's one to three inches deep will provide water for the finches.

- Place feeders near shrubs or trees: This will make the finches feel safe and encourage them to explore the feeder.

- Mount birdhouses out of reach: Place a birdhouse on a post in the middle of the yard, away from trees and buildings.

- Plant shrubby bushes: House Finches like to eat in bushes close to the ground, so planting bushes can help attract them.

- Hang a wreath: Hanging a wreath on your front door can also help attract House Finches.

## (8 ) Mourning Dove (Zenaida macroura):

- **Description:** A graceful dove with a slender tail and small head. They are common across North America, often seen perching on wires or foraging for seeds on the ground. Their flight is fast and straight, and their calls are soft and mournful coos. You can distinguish them from the Eurasian Collared-Dove by the lack of a black neck collar.

- **Range:** Found throughout most of North America, Central America, and parts of the Caribbean.

- **Diet:** Almost exclusively seed eaters, favoring hemp, wheat, foxtail, corn, pigweed, and ragweed.

- **Backyard Tips :**

- Scatter seeds like millet on the ground or feeders.
- Plant shrubs or evergreen trees for nesting sites.
- Keep cats indoors, as doves on the ground are vulnerable.
- Offer nesting cones before breeding season.

Mourning Dove

http://www.naturespicsonline.com/, CC BY-SA 2.5, via Wikimedia Commons

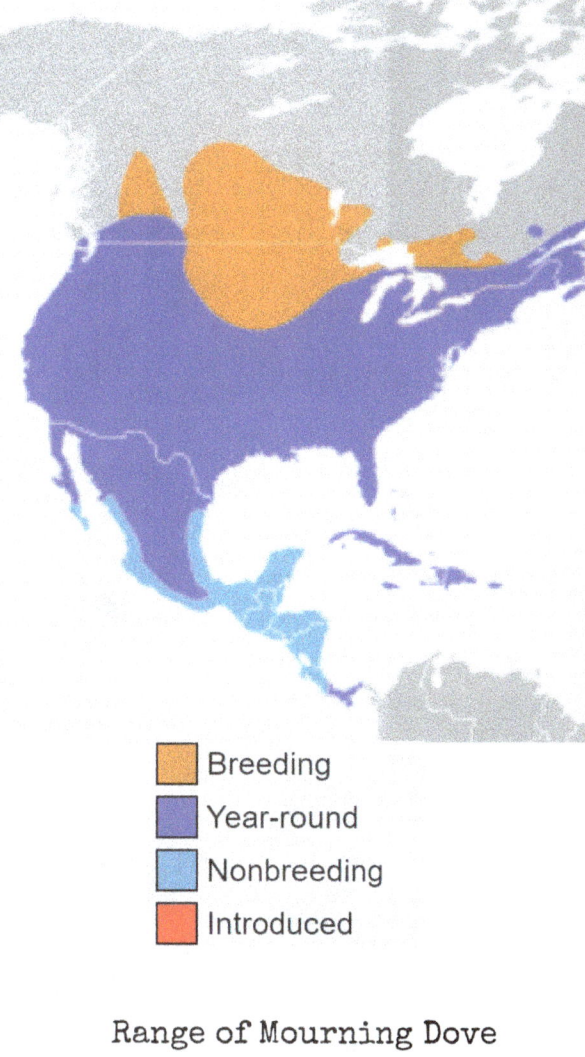

Range of Mourning Dove

By Jebbles — This file was derived from: BlankMap-World.svg;, CC0, https://commons.wikimedia.org/w/index.php?curid=108062078

### (9) Northern mockingbird (Mimus polyglottos):

- **Description:** Medium-sized gray songbird with a long tail, white wing patches, and white outer tail feathers. They prefer open areas with scattered shrubs and trees.

- **Range:** Found throughout most of North America, from southern Canada down to Mexico. Some northern populations may migrate short distances south during harsh winters. They are rarely seen in Europe.

- **Diet:** Omnivorous, eating a variety of insects, fruits, and even small vertebrates like lizards. In spring and summer, they consume more insects, while fall and winter see a shift towards fruits and berries.

- **Backyard Tips :**

    - Maintain an open lawn with scattered trees and shrubs.
    - Plant fruiting trees and bushes like mulberries, hawthorns, and blackberries.
    - Offer natural food sources like fruits and berries.
    - Avoid using pesticides, which can harm their insect prey.

Northern mockingbird

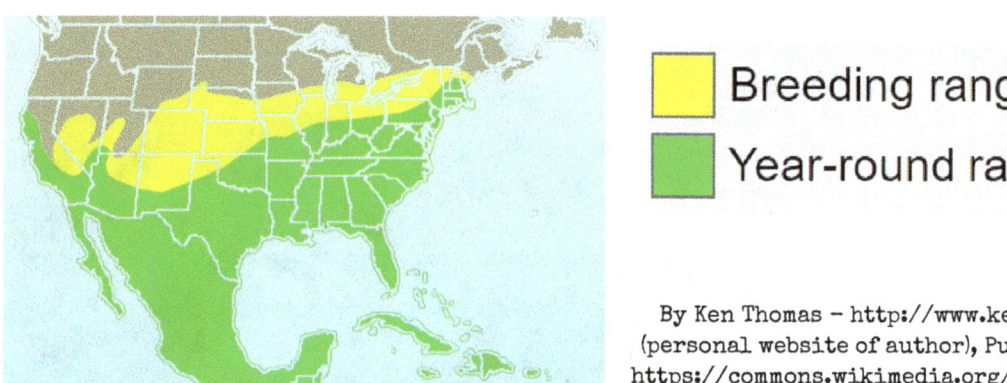

Range of Northern mockingbird

## (10) Blue Jay (Cyanocitta cristata):

- **Description:** A large, colorful songbird with a blue crest, black collar, and white underparts. They are intelligent and adaptable, common in woodlands and backyards.

- **Range:** Found throughout eastern and central North America, from southern Canada to Florida and Texas. They are permanent residents in most areas, but some eastern populations may migrate short distances south during harsh winters.

- **Diet:** Omnivorous, eating various foods, including acorns, nuts, seeds, fruits, insects, and even small vertebrates. They store food by hiding it to retrieve it later.

- **Backyard Tips :** Attract blue jays with tray or hopper feeders filled with peanuts, sunflower seeds, or suet. Offer birdbaths for them to drink from. Consider planting oak trees to provide a future food source.

Blue Jay

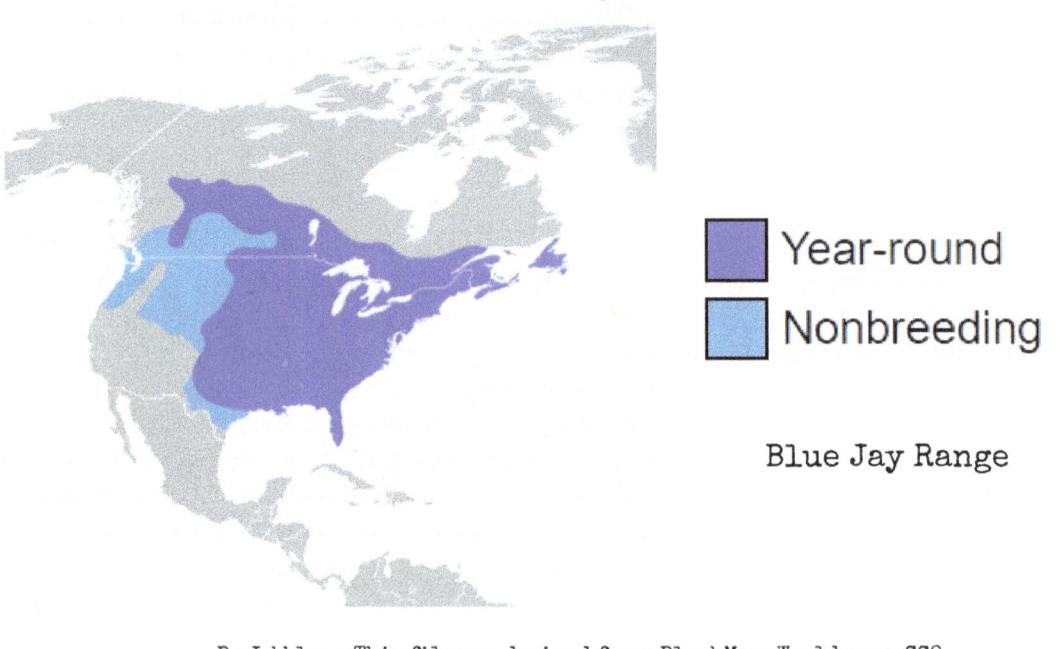

Blue Jay Range

By Jebbles - This file was derived from: BlankMap-World.svg;, CC0, https://commons.wikimedia.org/w/index.php?curid=108088972

## (11) White-breasted Nuthatch (Sitta carolinensis):

- **Description:** A small songbird with a white face and underside, bluish-gray back and wings, and a dark cap (black in males, gray in females). They are known for creeping down tree trunks headfirst and their distinctive "yank-yank" call.

- **Range:** Found throughout most of North America, from southern Canada to northern Florida and southern Mexico. They are year-round residents, even in cold areas.

- **Diet:** Primarily insects and spiders in summer, supplemented with seeds in winter. They store seeds in bark crevices to eat later.

- **Backyard Tips :**

    - Offer large nuts like peanuts, sunflower seeds, and suet.
    - Provide a shallow bird bath (1-2 inches deep) near trees or shrubs.
    - Consider a heated bath in northern winter.
    - Install a nest box with a predator guard before breeding season.
    - Maintain a yard with plenty of trees for foraging and shelter.

White-breasted Nuthatch

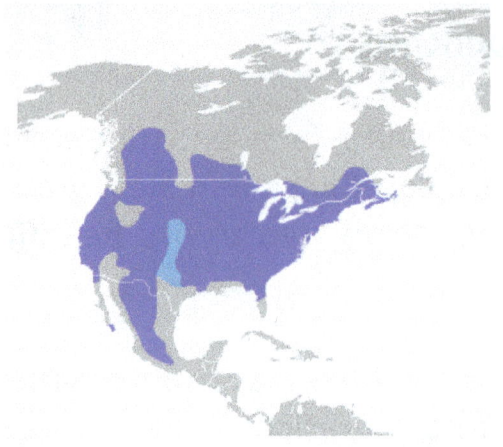
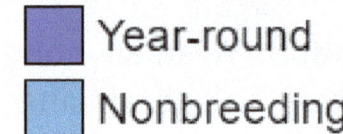

By Jebbles – This file was derived from: BlankMap-World.svg:, CC0, https://commons.wikimedia.org/w/index.php?curid=108088948

Range of White-breasted Nuthatch

## (12) Dark-eyed Junco (Junco hyemalis)

- **Description:** A small, sparrow-like bird with a gray hood and white belly (lighter in northern and eastern populations). Their bright white tail feathers that flash in flight make them easy to recognize.

- **Range:** Found throughout most of North America, breeding in coniferous or mixed-coniferous forests across Canada, the western U.S., and the Appalachians. In winter, they move to open woodlands, fields, parks, roadsides, and backyards. Some populations are short-distance migrants, while others travel long distances between breeding and wintering grounds.

- **Diet:** Primarily seeds and grains in winter, supplemented by insects, berries, and grass seeds in summer. They forage on the ground.

**Backyard Tips :**

- Food: Offer hulled sunflower seeds, white proso millet, cracked corn, thistle, or black-oil sunflower seeds on a low platform feeder or scattered on the ground.

- Water: Provide a shallow, heated bird bath near shrubs in winter.

- Shelter: Leave bushes and shrubs untrimmed for cover and consider offering roost boxes in winter.

- Plants: Plant shrubs with berries like Eastern Red Cedar, Choke Cherry, Elderberry, or Winterberry to provide a natural food source.

Dark-Eyed Juncos

Photo by Anish Lakkapragada on Unsplash

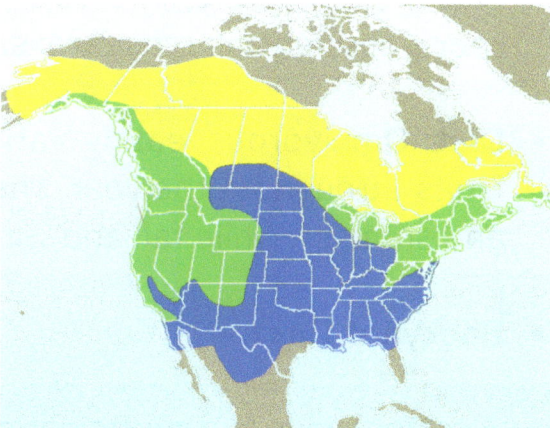

Dark-Eyed Juncos Range

By Ken Thomas - http://www.kenthomas.us (personal website of author), Public Domain, https://commons.wikimedia.org/w/index.php?curid=37191226

### (13) Spotted Towhee(Pipilo maculatus):

- **Description:** A medium-sized sparrow with a dark head and back, spotted wings, rusty sides, and striking red eyes. They forage on the ground, scratching in leaf litter for food. Their song is a simple trill.

- **Range:** Found across western North America, breeding from Alaska and southern Canada to California, Nevada, Arizona, Utah, Oregon, Washington, Idaho, and southern British Columbia. They are year-round residents in most areas.

- **Diet:** Omnivorous, eating various insects, seeds, berries, and small fruits throughout the year. Their diet leans towards insects in spring and summer, while fall and winter shift towards seeds and berries.

- **Backyard Tips :**

  - Scatter seeds like sunflower seeds, safflower, white millet, peanuts, and cracked corn on the ground near shrubs.
  - Offer a shallow bird bath with moving water near brushy areas.
  - Maintain natural areas in your yard with low-hanging shrubs and leaf litter for cover.

Spotted Towhee

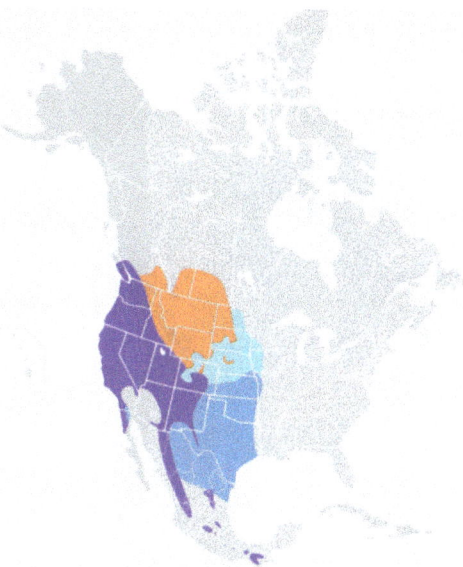

By Cephas - Bartos Smith, S. and J. S. Greenlaw. 2015. Spotted Towhee (Pipilo maculatus), version 2.0. In The Birds of North America (P. G. Rodewald, Editor). Cornell Lab of Ornithology, Ithaca, NY, USA. https://doi-org.acces.bibl.ulaval.ca/10.2173/bna.263, CC BY-SA 4.0, https://commons.wikimedia.org/w/index.php?curid=68518010

Range of spotted towhee

### (14) Downy Woodpecker (Dryobates pubescens)

- **Description:** The smallest woodpecker in North America, with a short bill, white belly, black back with white streaks and spots, and a red patch on the back of the male's head (absent in females).

- **Range:** Found throughout most of North America, in forested areas (mainly deciduous) except for the southwestern deserts and northern tundra. Some northern populations may migrate short distances south in winter.

- **Diet:** Primarily insects, especially wood-boring beetles, eat fruits, seeds, and nuts.

**Backyard Tips :**

- Offer suet, peanuts, peanut butter, and seeds in feeders near mature trees.
- Provide a shallow dish of water for drinking and bathing.
- Create a natural habitat with trees, snags, and brush piles. Offer nest boxes with small entrance holes.

Downy Woodpecker

Image by <a href="https://pixabay.com/users/veronika_andrews-16688553/?utm_source=link-attribution&utm_medium=referral&utm_campaign=image&utm_content=7767225">Veronika Andrews</a> from <a href="https://pixabay.com/?utm_source=link-attribution&utm_medium=referral&utm_campaign=image&utm_content=7767225">Pixabay</a>

Approximate distribution map

■ Year-round

Range of Downy Woodpecker

By Jebbles - This file was derived from: BlankMap-World.svg:, CC0, https://commons.wikimedia.org/w/index.php?curid=108042849

## (15) Ruby-throated Hummingbird (Archilochus colubris):

- **Description:** The only hummingbird regularly breeding in eastern North America. Tiny with a long bill, males have a bright red throat (gorget), while females have a white throat.

- **Range:** Breeds in eastern North America, from southern Canada to Florida and Texas. Winters in Central America and Mexico.

- **Diet:** Primarily nectar from flowers, but also eats small insects like flies, gnats, and aphids for protein.

**Backyard Tips:**

- Hang feeders with a 1:4 ratio sugar-water solution (sugar to water). Avoid red dye and artificial sweeteners.
- Plant red or orange flowers like columbine, bee balm, honeysuckle, or impatiens.
- Provide perches and shelter near feeders with trees or shrubs.
- Place feeders away from cats (at least 15ft above ground).

Ruby-throated Hummingbird

Image by <a href="https://pixabay.com/users/publicdomainimages-327722/?utm_source=link-attribution&utm_medium=referral&utm_campaign=image&utm_content=386847">PublicDomainImages</a> from <a href="https://pixabay.com//?utm_source=link-attribution&utm_medium=referral&utm_campaign=image&utm_content=386847">Pixabay</a>

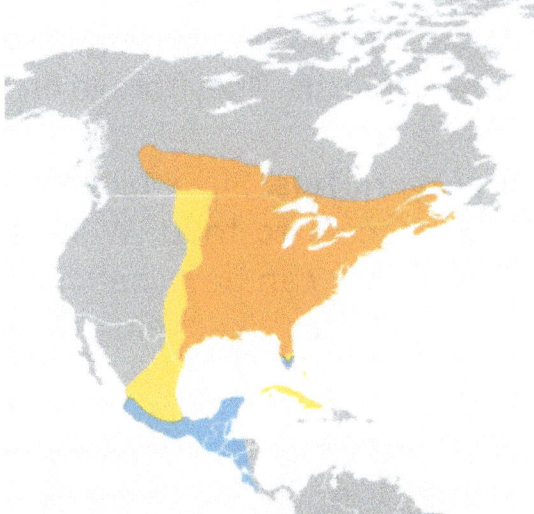

Ruby-throated Hummingbird

By Jebbles - This file was derived from: BlankMap-World.svg:, CC0, https://commons.wikimedia.org/w/index.php?curid=108088882

## (16) Black-billed Magpie ( Pica hudsonia ):

- **Description:** A large, black and white bird with a long tail and iridescent blue-green highlights on the wings and tail. They are intelligent and social birds.

- **Range:** Found in western North America, from Alaska to northern California and Texas.

- **Diet:** Omnivorous, eating insects, worms, carrion, fruits, seeds, and small animals. They forage on the ground.

- **Backyard Tips:** Black-billed magpies are attracted to backyards with easy access to food. While some methods may attempt to deter them, they can be beneficial insectivores. Consider offering natural food sources like fruits and leaving some grubs or worms in the yard.

Black-billed Magpie

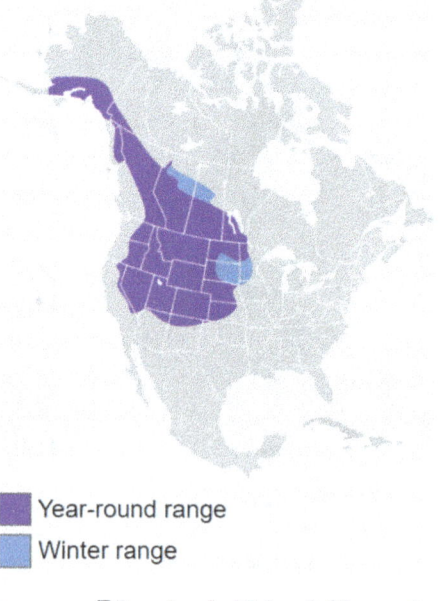

Range-Black-billed Magpie

By Cephas - Trost, C. H. (1999). Black-billed Magpie (Pica hudsonia), version 2.0. In The Birds of North America (A. F. Poole and F. B. Gill, Editors). Cornell Lab of Ornithology, Ithaca, NY, USA. https://doi-org.acces.bibl.ulaval.ca/10.2173/bna.389, CC BY-SA 4.0, https://commons.wikimedia.org/w/index.php?curid=69347862

## (17) Baltimore Oriole ( Icterus galbula) :

- **Description:** Medium-sized blackbird with a thick bill and long legs. Males are black and orange, while females are duller orange and yellow.

- **Range:** Breeds in eastern North America from southern Canada to the Gulf Coast, winters in Mexico, Central America, and northern South America.

- **Diet:** Omnivorous, eating insects, fruits, nectar, and sap. They are known for their sweet tooth and love for grape jelly.

**Backyard Tips:**

- Offer oranges, grape jelly (in moderation), sugar water, and mealworms.
- Plant dark berries and nectar-producing flowers like trumpet vine.
- Hang oriole feeders with large perches in a quiet, open area near a birdbath.
- Put feeders out in mid-March and remove them in late fall.

Baltimore Oriole

Image by <a href="https://pixabay.com/users/wpresnel2024-39450766/?utm_source=link-attribution&utm_medium=referral&utm_campaign=image&utm_content=8253731">Wayne Presnell</a> from <a href="https://pixabay.com//?utm_source=link-attribution&utm_medium=referral&utm_campaign=image&utm_content=8253731">Pixabay</a>

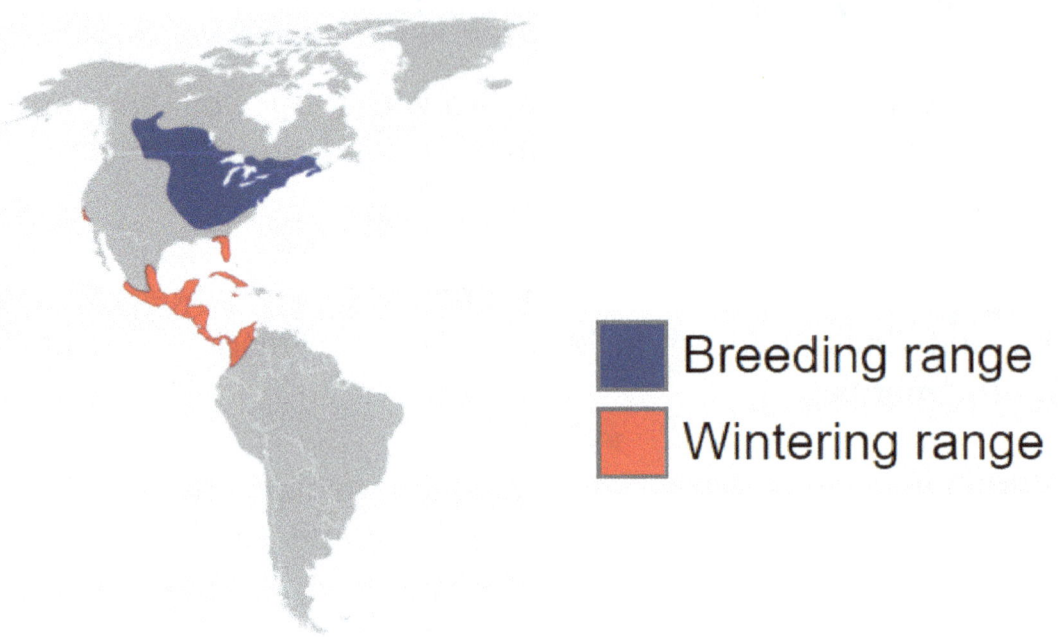

Range-Baltimore oriole

By Cephas - Own work, CC BY-SA 3.0, https://commons.wikimedia.org/w/index.php?curid=6100095

## (18) American Crow (Corvus brachyrhynchos)

- **Description:** Large, intelligent, all-black bird with a harsh "caw" call.

- **Range:** Found throughout most of North America, from Alaska and Canada to Mexico.

- **Diet:** Omnivorous, eating various plant and animal foods, including seeds, fruits, insects, small animals, carrion, and garbage.

- **Backyard Tips:** While not common feeder birds, crows may visit yards with scattered peanuts, compost piles, or open areas near trees. They also appreciate a shallow birdbath for drinking and bathing.

American Crow

Range of American Crow
By Jack · talk · – self map, Public Domain, https://commons.wikimedia.org/w/index.php?curid=2442138

### (19) Common Grackle (Quiscalus quiscula):

- **Description:** Large blackbird with a long, tapered bill, long legs, and a long tail that folds into a V-shape during flight. Their bodies have a glossy, iridescent sheen.

- **Range:** Found throughout eastern North America east of the Rockies, breeding in southern Canada and wintering south to the Great Lakes and New England.

- **Diet:** Omnivorous, eating seeds, grains, fruits, insects, and even small animals. They forage on the ground and may follow plows or raid nests for food.

- **Backyard Tips:** While not typically feeder birds, common grackles may visit yards with scattered seeds or grains on the ground. Offering food on the ground can help keep them from dominating feeders used by smaller birds. However, avoid leaving out too much seed to prevent attracting rodents.

Common Grackle

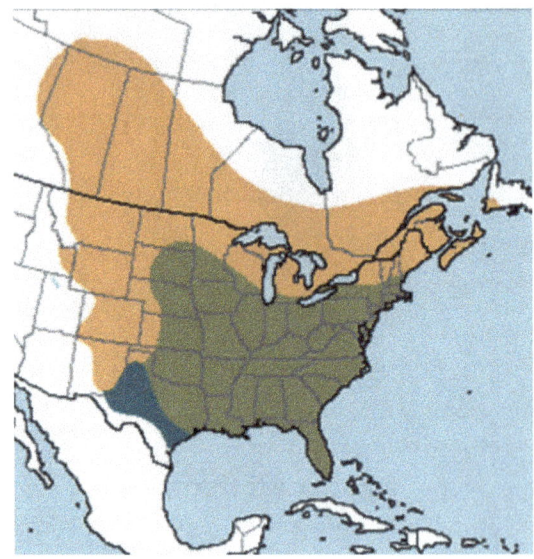

Range-Common Gracklee

Image by <a href="https://pixabay.com/users/bernell-2855442/?utm_source=link-attribution&utm_medium=referral&utm_campaign=image&utm_content=5339982">Bernell MacDonald</a> from <a href="https://pixabay.com//?utm_source=link-attribution&utm_medium=referral&utm_campaign=image&utm_content=5339982">Pixabay</a>

### (20) Northern flicker (Colaptes auratus):

- **Description:** Large woodpecker with brown bodies, black-scalloped feathers, and a curved bill. In flight, they show a flash of yellow (east) or red (west) on their wings and a white rump.

- **Range:** Found throughout most of North America, in woodlands, forests, and suburbs.

- **Diet:** Primarily insects, especially ants and beetles, but also eats fruits, seeds, and nuts. They forage on the ground as well as on trees.

**Backyard Tips:**

- Offer food like peanut hearts, suet, or seed on a platform feeder or ground.
- Provide a nest box mounted high above the ground.
- Plant native plants with different heights to create a natural habitat with cover and food sources.
- Leave dead trees standing for nesting sites.
- Offer a shallow water source for drinking.

Northern flicker

northern flicker or common flicker
(Colaptes auratus)

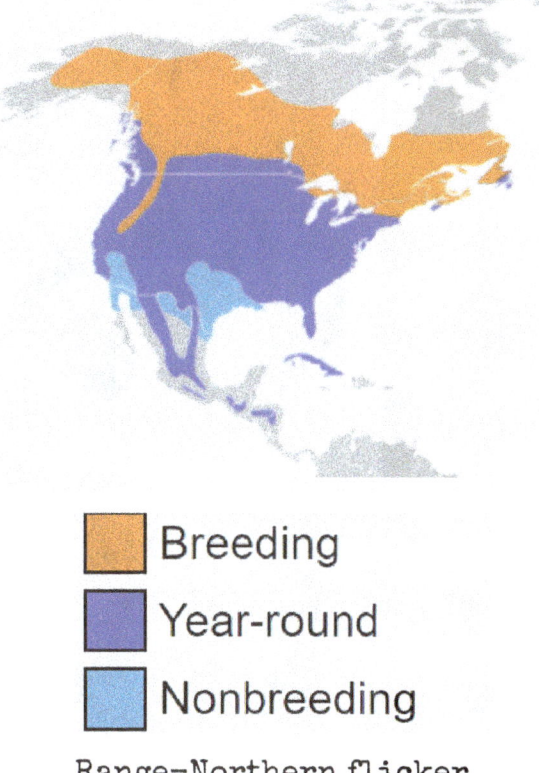

Range–Northern flicker

Welcome to the exciting world of documenting your backyard birding adventures! This chapter equips you with the tools to keep a comprehensive record of the feathered friends you encounter.

## Keeping a Bird Journal: Recording Your Observations

IA bird journal is your personal treasure trove of birding experiences. It's a place to capture details about the birds you see, helping you improve your identification skills and relive special moments. Here's what to include:

| DETAIL | DESCRIPTION | EXAMPLE |
|---|---|---|
| Date & Time | Note the date and time of your observation. | May 17, 2024, Morning (8:00 AM) |
| Location | Specify the location within your yard. | Backyard feeder near maple tree |
| Weather | Briefly mention weather conditions. | Sunny, light breeze |
| Bird Description | Describe the bird's appearance and notable features. | Medium-sized bird with black and white plumage. Distinctive long tail. Bright red patch on the back of its head (male). |
| Behavior | Describe the bird's activity during observation. | Singing loudly from a high branch, then flew down to feeder and perched on the edge. |
| Additional Notes | Include any other pertinent details. | Heard a loud "caw" call before spotting the bird. |

**Tips:**

- Carry a small notebook or use a birding app to record observations on the go.
- Sketch the bird or take a quick photo to jog your memory later.
- Include reference materials like field guides or online resources in your notes.

# Bird Sketching and Photography Tips

## Attracting Birds for Close-Up Photos:

| TECHNIQUE | DESCRIPTION |
|---|---|
| Set up feeders and birdbaths | Offer a variety of food and water sources to attract birds close to your viewing area. |
| Create a natural habitat | Plant native trees, shrubs, and flowers to provide birds with food, cover, and nesting sites. |
| Stay still and quiet | Be patient and maintain a distance that doesn't disturb the birds. |
| Use a blind | Consider building a small, camouflaged hide to get closer views without startling the birds. |

## Basic Bird Photography Techniques:

| TECHNIQUE | DESCRIPTION |
|---|---|
| Invest in a good zoom lens | Capture close-up shots without disturbing the birds. |
| Focus on lighting | Early mornings and late afternoons provide the best natural light. |
| Adjust camera settings | Experiment with aperture, shutter speed, and ISO for well-exposed photos. |
| Take multiple shots | Burst mode helps capture fleeting moments. |
| Edit your photos | Enhance clarity, color balance, and composition using basic editing software. |

# Building a Life List: Tracking the Birds You've Seen

A life list is a personal record of all the bird species you've identified. It's a way to track progress and celebrate achievements. Here's how:

| STEP | DESCRIPTION |
|---|---|
| Use a checklist or app | Track sightings with region-specific checklists. |
| Document sightings | Record each species in your bird journal or chosen tracking method. |
| Update regularly | Add new birds as you encounter them. |
| Share your list | Connect with other birders online or in local clubs. |

Creating a bird identification record is an ongoing process. The more you observe, sketch, photograph, and document, the deeper your connection with the fascinating world of birds will become!

## Real-Time Examples: Bird Journal Entries :

Here are examples of journal entries for three different birds to illustrate how to document your observations:

### Example 1: Northern Cardinal

| DETAIL | DESCRIPTION | EXAMPLE |
|---|---|---|
| Date & Time | Note the date and time of your observation. | May 18, 2024, Afternoon (3:00 PM) |

## Example 1: Northern Cardinal

| DETAIL | DESCRIPTION | EXAMPLE |
|---|---|---|
| Location | Specify the location within your yard. | Near birdbath under oak tree |
| Weather | Briefly mention weather conditions. | Partly cloudy, mild temperature |
| Bird Description | Describe the bird's appearance and notable features. | Bright red plumage, black face mask around beak (male) |
| Behavior | Describe the bird's activity during observation. | Hopping on the ground, pecking at seeds |
| Additional Notes | Include any other pertinent details. | Heard a melodious whistle-like song |

## Example 2: American Goldfinch

| DETAIL | DESCRIPTION | EXAMPLE |
|---|---|---|
| Date & Time | Note the date and time of your observation. | May 19, 2024, Morning (7:30 AM) |
| Location | Specify the location within your yard. | At the thistle feeder in the garden |
| Weather | Briefly mention weather conditions. | Sunny, calm |
| Bird Description | Describe the bird's appearance and notable features. | Bright yellow body, black wings with white markings (male) |
| Behavior | Describe the bird's activity during observation. | Clinging to the feeder, picking at thistle seeds |
| Additional Notes | Include any other pertinent details. | Observed fluttering flight pattern |

## Example 3 : Blue Jay

| DETAIL | DESCRIPTION | EXAMPLE |
|---|---|---|
| Date & Time | Note the date and time of your observation. | May 20, 2024, Midday (12:00 PM) |
| Location | Specify the location within your yard. | On the fence near the maple tree |
| Weather | Briefly mention weather conditions. | Overcast, light drizzle |
| Bird Description | Describe the bird's appearance and notable features. | Blue upperparts, white underparts, black necklace |
| Behavior | Describe the bird's activity during observation. | Calling loudly, flying between fence and tree |
| Additional Notes | Include any other pertinent details. | Noted aggressive behavior towards smaller birds |

## 20 Most Famous Backyard Birds: Identification Guide

Here's a table of 20 of North America's most common backyard birds, including their distinctive features, typical habitats, and when they are most often seen. This will help you quickly identify these birds during your birdwatching sessions.

| BIRD SPECIES | DISTINCTIVE FEATURE | WHEN SEEN | WHERE FOUND | REGIONS WITH MAXIMUM CHANCES |
|---|---|---|---|---|
| Northern Cardinal | Bright red plumage (male), red beak | Year-round | Shrubs, gardens, and wooded edges | Eastern and Central U.S. |
| American Goldfinch | Bright yellow body, black wings (male) | Late spring to early fall | Open fields, gardens, and feeders | Throughout U.S. and Southern Canada |
| Blue Jay | Blue upperparts, white underparts, black necklace | Year-round | Forest edges, parks, and backyards | Eastern and Central U.S. |
| Black-capped Chickadee | Black cap and bib, white cheeks | Year-round | Woodlands, parks, and feeders | Northern U.S. and Southern Canada |

| BIRD SPECIES | DISTINCTIVE FEATURE | WHEN SEEN | WHERE FOUND | REGIONS WITH MAXIMUM CHANCES |
|---|---|---|---|---|
| Mourning Dove | Slender, grayish-brown body, long pointed tail | Year-round | Open grounds and urban areas | Throughout U.S. |
| American Robin | Reddish-orange breast | Spring to fall | Lawns, gardens, and parks | Throughout U.S. and Canada |
| House Sparrow | Chunky body, gray head (male), brown and black streaks | Year-round | Urban and suburban areas | Throughout U.S. and Canada |
| Downy Woodpecker | Small size, black and white plumage, red patch on head (male) | Year-round | Deciduous forests and woodlots | Throughout U.S. and Canada |
| House Finch | Red head and chest (male), streaked brown body | Year-round | Urban areas, backyards, and parks | Western U.S., spread to Eastern U.S. |
| European Starling | Iridescent black plumage with speckles | Year-round | Urban areas and open fields | Throughout U.S. and Canada |
| Northern Mockingbird | Gray body, white wing patches | Year-round | Open areas with shrubs and trees | Southern and Eastern U.S. |
| Red-winged Blackbird | Black body, red and yellow shoulder patches (male) | Spring to fall | Wetlands and marshes | Throughout U.S. |
| White-breasted Nuthatch | White face and underparts, black cap | Year-round | Deciduous forests and feeders | Throughout U.S. and Southern Canada |
| Eastern Bluebird | Bright blue upperparts, rusty chest | Spring to fall | Open woodlands and farmlands | Eastern and Central U.S. |
| Song Sparrow | Streaked brown plumage, distinctive central breast spot | Year-round | Shrublands, gardens, and wetlands | Throughout U.S. and Canada |
| Tufted Titmouse | Gray crest, large black eyes, rusty flanks | Year-round | Deciduous forests and feeders | Eastern U.S. |
| Dark-eyed Junco | Dark gray or brownish body, white belly | Winter | Woodlands and suburban areas | Northern U.S. and Canada in summer; Throughout U.S. in winter |
| American Crow | All black, large and noisy | Year-round | Open areas and woodlands | Throughout U.S. and Canada |
| Baltimore Oriole | Bright orange and black plumage (male) | Late spring to summer | Deciduous trees and gardens | Eastern U.S. and Southern Canada |
| Ruby-throated Hummingbird | Bright red throat (male), iridescent green back | Late spring to early fall | Gardens and wood edges | Eastern U.S. and Southern Canada |

Use this table to enhance your birdwatching experience. It will help you identify and appreciate the diverse bird species visiting your backyard. Happy birding!

# Chapter 5: DIY Birdhouses, Feeders & Seed Mixes

In this chapter, you will transform your backyard into a haven for feathered friends! We'll guide you through creating birdhouses and feeders using everyday materials and concocting nutritious seed mixes that cater to different bird species.

## Birdhouses Basics

Birdhouses play an important role in North American bird conservation. By providing safe havens for cavity-nesting birds, we offer them alternative nesting sites and boost their breeding success. Birdhouses also provide an opportunity to track bird populations and breeding activity. Everyone is encouraged to consider putting up a birdhouse in their backyard to contribute to bird conservation in their neighborhood.

### Key Considerations for Birdhouse Design

- **Target Bird:** Different bird species have different needs. Research cavity-nesting birds in your area and choose a design that caters to their size.

- **Size Required**: The internal cavity and entrance hole size are crucial. A house that's too small can be cramped and uncomfortable, while a hole that's too large might attract unwanted guests like squirrels or starlings. Considering these factors, you create a comfortable space for your feathered friends.

- **Material matters:** Opt for breathable materials like untreated wood, which provide insulation and ventilation. Avoid metal or plastic, which can trap heat and moisture.

- **Safety first**: Ensuring the birdhouse is sturdy and secure is crucial to prevent tipping or falling. Avoid sharp edges or protruding nails inside, as these could harm the birds. You show your care and concern for the birds' well-being by prioritizing safety.

- **Ventilation is critical**: Proper air circulation helps regulate temperature and prevents moisture build-up. Consider small ventilation holes near the roof eaves.

- **Cleanliness counts**: Design your birdhouse with a removable roof or hinged front for easy cleaning after the nesting season.

- **Predators beware:** Avoid features like perches that predators can use to access the chicks. You can even add predator baffles around the mounting pole for extra security.

- **Location**: Place the birdhouse in a sheltered spot away from direct sunlight and strong winds. Consider the bird species' preference for sun or shade.

## Different Types of Birdhouses: A Detailed Guide for Bird Enthusiasts

### 1. Nest Boxes

- **Made from** Untreated wood (ideally cedar, pine) or recycled plastic.
- **Where to place:** Mounted on poles, trees, fences, or buildings in open areas.
- **For birds:** Cavity nesters like chickadees, wrens, bluebirds, and nuthatches.

- **Advantages:** Simple design, easy to monitor and clean, promotes breeding success in cavity-limited habitats.
- **Disadvantages:** It can be usurped by aggressive house sparrows and may require predator baffles.

Details:

- **Size:** Varies depending on the target bird. A chickadee house typically has a 1.25-inch entrance hole and a 4x4-inch base, while a bluebird house might have a 1.5-inch hole and a 5x5-inch base.
- **Ventilation:** Small holes near the roof for air circulation.
- **Cleaning:** Removable roof or hinged front for easy access.

Nest Box

## 2. Wren Houses

- **Made from** Wood, gourds, or recycled materials.
- **Where to place:** Mounted on trees, fences, or posts in semi-shaded areas.
- **For birds:** Wrens, especially house wrens and Bewick's wrens.
- **Advantages:** A small entrance hole discourages larger birds and provides a haven for wrens.
- **Disadvantages:** It can be messy due to wren nesting habits and may attract competition from other wren species.

Details:

- **Size:** Smaller than chickadee houses, with a 1-inch entrance hole and a 4x4-inch base.
- **Entrance:** Often positioned on the side of the house, not the front.
- **Ventilation:** Small holes near the roof for air circulation.
- **Cleaning:** Removable top or hinged front for easy access after nesting season.

Wren House

## 3. Bluebird Houses

- **Made from:** Untreated wood (cedar, pine) with a metal predator guard.
- **Where to place:** Mounted on poles in open areas with minimal obstructions, at least 4-6 feet above the ground.
- **For birds:** Eastern and Western Bluebirds.
- **Advantages:** Large size and open design deter house sparrows, and predator guard provides extra security.
- **Disadvantages:** Requiring specific sun exposure placement may attract competition from other bluebird families.

Details:

- **Size:** Slightly larger than chickadee houses, with a 1.5-inch entrance hole and a 5x5-inch base.
- **Ventilation:** Small holes near the roof for air circulation.
- **Cleaning:** Removable roof or hinged front for easy access after nesting season.

Bluebird House

## 4. Robin Platforms

- **Made from** Untreated wood or recycled materials with a rough surface for grip.
- **Where to place:** Mounted on a sturdy post, fence, or building in a shaded location.
- **For birds:** Robins, American robins in particular.
- **Advantages:** Open platform design caters to robins' preference for building cup nests.
- **Disadvantages:** Exposed nests may be vulnerable to predators, platform design doesn't offer insulation.

Details:

- **Size:** Larger than nest boxes, with a base of at least 6x6 inches to accommodate robin nests.
- **Surface:** Rough wood or added twigs to provide grip for nesting materials.
- **Drainage:** Sloped design or small holes to allow for rainwater drainage.

Robin Platforms

## 5. Purple Martin Houses

- **Made from** Wood or sturdy plastic with multiple compartments.
- **Where to place:** Mounted on high poles in open areas, away from trees and buildings.
- **For birds:** Purple martins are colonial birds that nest in large groups.
- **Advantages:** Multi-compartment design attracts large colonies of purple martins, which is excellent for insect control.
- **Disadvantages:** Requires significant maintenance and may attract competition from starlings or house sparrows.

Details:

- **Size:** Varies depending on the number of compartments, with individual compartments similar to bluebird house dimensions.
- **Entrance Holes:** Multiple entrances, one for each compartment.
- **Ventilation:** Proper air circulation is crucial due to the number of nesting birds.
- **Cleaning:** Removable compartments for thorough cleaning after the nesting season.

Photo by Brad Weaver on Unsplash

Purple Martin Houses

## 6. Flicker Houses

- **Made from:** Wood with a deep interior cavity.
- **Where to place:** Mounted on mature trees with rough bark in open woodlands.
- **For birds:** Northern Flickers, large woodpeckers that nest in cavities.
- **Advantages:** Deep cavity caters to the flicker's long body, design discourages smaller birds.
- **Disadvantages:** Large size may attract unwanted predators, requires mounting on a sturdy tree.

Details:

- **Size:** Significantly larger than chickadee houses, with a 2-inch entrance hole and a base of at least 6x6 inches to accommodate the flicker's depth requirement.
- **Ventilation:** Small holes near the roof for air circulation.
- **Cleaning:** Removable roof or hinged front for easy access after nesting season.

Flicker House

## 6. Flicker Houses

- **Made from:** Wood with a deep interior cavity.
- **Where to place:** Mounted on mature trees with rough bark in open woodlands.
- **For birds:** Northern Flickers, large woodpeckers that nest in cavities.
- **Advantages:** Deep cavity caters to the flicker's long body, design discourages smaller birds.
- **Disadvantages:** Large size may attract unwanted predators, requires mounting on a sturdy tree.

Details:

- **Size:** Significantly larger than chickadee houses, with a 2-inch entrance hole and a base of at least 6x6 inches to accommodate the flicker's depth requirement.
- **Ventilation:** Small holes near the roof for air circulation.
- **Cleaning:** Removable roof or hinged front for easy access after nesting season.

Flicker House

# 7. Kestrel Boxes

- **Made from** Wood with a large entrance hole and a rough landing area.
- **Where to place:** Mounted on high poles or buildings in open areas with clear views.
- **For birds:** American Kestrels, small falcons that nest in cavities.
- **Advantages:** Large entrances and landing areas cater to the kestrel's hunting style.
- **Disadvantages:** It requires specific placement for hunting visibility and may attract competition from other cavity-nesting birds.

Details:

- **Size:** Larger than bluebird houses, with a 3-inch entrance hole and a base of at least 8x8 inches.
- **Landing Perch:** A roughened wooden platform is below the entrance for landing and surveying the surroundings.
- **Ventilation:** Small holes near the roof for air circulation.
- **Cleaning:** Removable roof or hinged front for easy access after nesting season.

Kestrel Box

## 8. Wood Duck Houses

- **Made from** Wood with predator guards and predator baffles.
- **Where to place:** Mounted on sturdy posts or trees near water sources, with the entrance facing the water.
- **For birds:** Wood Ducks, cavity-nesting waterfowl that prefer elevated nesting sites.
- **Advantages:** Elevated design protects ducklings from predators, and predator guards and baffles offer additional security.
- **Disadvantages:** It requires placement near water and may not be suitable for all backyards.

Details:
- **Size:** Larger than nest boxes, with a 4-inch entrance hole at least 12 inches above the base (to allow ducklings to jump down safely) and a base of at least 8x8 inches.
- **Rough Landing:** Roughened wood around the entrance for ducklings to grip.
- **Ventilation:** Small holes near the roof for air circulation.
- **Drainage:** Sloped roof design to prevent water accumulation.
- **Cleaning:** Removable roof or hinged front for easy access after nesting season.

Wood Duck Houses

## 9. Gourd Houses

- **Made from:** Natural gourds (dried, hollowed-out gourds) or imitation gourds made from wood or plastic.
- **Where to place:** Mounted on sturdy poles or fences in open areas with some sun exposure.
- **For birds:** Many cavity-nesting bird species, including wrens, bluebirds, chickadees, and swallows.
- **Advantages:** Natural material can be aesthetically pleasing, some gourds have multiple compartments for attracting different species.
- **Disadvantages:** Real gourds may require more maintenance to prevent rotting and may not be as durable as wooden houses.

Details:
- **Size:** This varies depending on the type of gourd and target bird species. However, it is generally similar in size to standard nest boxes or wren houses.
- **Entrance Holes**: This may require creating an entrance hole of the appropriate size for the target bird species.
- **Ventilation**: Small drainage holes are important, especially for natural gourds.
- **Cleaning:** The top of the gourd can often be removed for cleaning after the nesting season.

Gourd House

## 10. Log Homes

- **Made from:** Sections of hollowed-out logs or branches with natural cavities.
- **Where to place:** Mounted on sturdy poles or trees in wooded areas, mimicking natural nesting sites.
- **For birds:** Woodpeckers, nuthatches, chickadees, and other cavity-nesting birds that prefer natural cavities.
- **Advantages:** Provides a natural nesting environment for birds accustomed to using cavities in trees or logs.
- **Disadvantages:** It may be difficult to find or create, can be heavy, and require sturdy mounting.

Details:

- **Size:** The size varies depending on the size of the natural log section, but it is generally similar to that of standard nest boxes.
- **Entrance Holes**: Existing natural cavity openings can be used, or an entrance hole of the appropriate size can be created on the side of the log.
- **Ventilation**: Natural ventilation through cracks and crevices in the log.
- **Cleaning**: It may be difficult to clean thoroughly due to the natural cavities, but some designs have removable backs for access.

Log Bird House

# Birdhouse Placement and Maintenance

## Best Locations for Different Bird Species

Different bird species have unique nesting site preferences. Choosing the right location for your birdhouse is crucial for attracting the desired birds and ensuring their safety and comfort.

| BIRD SPECIES | IDEAL LOCATION | SPECIFIC REQUIREMENTS |
|---|---|---|
| Chickadees | Open areas, garden edges | 4-6 feet above ground, facing away from prevailing winds |
| Bluebirds | Open fields, meadows | 4-6 feet above ground, 100 feet apart from each other |
| Wrens | Semi-shaded areas, gardens | 4-10 feet above ground, near shrubs or small trees |
| Purple Martins | Open areas, near water | 12-20 feet above ground, colony housing |
| Robins | Shaded locations, garden edges | 6-15 feet above ground, open platform |
| Wood Ducks | Near water sources, wooded areas | 6-30 feet above ground, facing water |
| Kestrels | Open fields, farmland | 10-30 feet above ground, clear line of sight |
| Flickers | Mature trees, open woodlands | 6-20 feet above ground, facing open area |

## Height and Orientation Guidelines

Proper height and orientation of birdhouses play a significant role in attracting birds and protecting them from predators and adverse weather.

| BIRD SPECIES | RECOMMENDED HEIGHT (FEET) | ORIENTATION (ENTRANCE DIRECTION) |
|---|---|---|
| Chickadees | 4-6 | East or southeast |
| Bluebirds | 4-6 | East |
| Wrens | 4-10 | Varies, slightly shaded |
| Purple Martins | 12-20 | Open, facing away from prevailing winds |
| Robins | 6-15 | Varies, shaded areas |
| Wood Ducks | 6-30 | Facing water |
| Kestrels | 10-30 | South or east |
| Flickers | 6-20 | Facing open area |

## Seasonal Maintenance Tips

Regular maintenance of birdhouses ensures they remain safe and attractive for birds year-round.

1. **Spring Preparation:**

    - **Clean birdhouses:** Remove old nests and debris and check for damage.
    - **Repair and reinforce:** Fix structural issues and securely mount the birdhouse.
    - **Install fresh nesting materials:** Some species, like bluebirds, may appreciate a small amount of soft material.

| BIRD SPECIES | RECOMMENDED HEIGHT (FEET) | ORIENTATION (ENTRANCE DIRECTION) |
|---|---|---|
| Chickadees | 4-6 | East or southeast |
| Bluebirds | 4-6 | East |
| Wrens | 4-10 | Varies, slightly shaded |
| Purple Martins | 12-20 | Open, facing away from prevailing winds |
| Robins | 6-15 | Varies, shaded areas |
| Wood Ducks | 6-30 | Facing water |
| Kestrels | 10-30 | South or east |
| Flickers | 6-20 | Facing open area |

## Seasonal Maintenance Tips

Regular maintenance of birdhouses ensures they remain safe and attractive for birds year-round.

### Spring Preparation:

- **Clean birdhouses:** Remove old nests and debris and check for damage.
- **Repair and reinforce:** Fix structural issues and securely mount the birdhouse.
- **Install fresh nesting materials:** Some species, like bluebirds, may appreciate a small amount of soft material.

**Summer Care:**

- **Monitor for activity:** Monitor nesting birds and check for signs of predators.
- **Provide water sources:** Ensure nearby water sources are available and clean.

**Autumn Cleaning:**

- **Post-nesting cleanup:** Remove any remaining nesting material to prevent mold and parasites.
- **Inspect for wear:** Check for and repair any weather damage from the summer months.

**Winter Preparation:**

- **Insulate if necessary:** In colder climates, add insulation to birdhouses to help overwintering species.
- **Check mounting stability:** Ensure birdhouses are secure against winter storms.

## Addressing Common Problems

Predators: Identifying and Deterring Common Threats
Birdhouses can attract predators like cats, snakes, raccoons, and larger birds. Implementing deterrent measures is crucial for the safety of nesting birds.

**Cats and Raccoons:**
- **Predator guards**: Install baffles or predator guards around the mounting poles.
- **Location**: Avoid placing birdhouses near overhanging branches or structures predators can climb.

**Snakes:**

- **Baffles:** Use metal baffles on poles to prevent snakes from climbing.
- **Monitor regularly:** Check for snake activity around birdhouses.

**Larger Birds:**

- **Entrance hole size:** To prevent larger birds from entering, ensure the entrance hole size is appropriate for the target species.
- **Positioning:** Place birdhouses away from areas frequented by larger predatory birds.

## Competition: Ensuring Adequate Space and Resources

Birdhouses sometimes attract unwanted competition from non-native species like house sparrows and starlings.

**Proper Spacing:**

- **Spacing guidelines**: Follow species-specific spacing guidelines to reduce competition.
- **Multiple birdhouses**: Provide several birdhouses with appropriate spacing to accommodate different species.

**Monitoring and Intervention:**

- **Regular checks**: Monitor birdhouses regularly for signs of aggressive competition.
- **Manage invasive species**: Remove non-native species nests if they threaten native birds.

## Installing Predator Guards and Monitoring Birdhouse Activity

Installing predator guards and monitoring birdhouse activity can significantly increase the success rate of nesting birds.

### Installing Predator Guards:
- **Types of guards:** Use cone-shaped or cylindrical baffles on poles for deer climbing predators.
- **Placement:** Ensure guards are placed at a height that prevents predators from reaching the birdhouse.

### Monitoring Activity:
- **Regular observation:** Check birdhouses weekly during the nesting season for signs of predators or competition.
- **Camera installation:** Consider installing wildlife cameras to monitor birdhouse activity remotely.

### Summary Table: Birdhouse Maintenance Schedule

| SEASON | ACTIVITY | DETAILS |
|---|---|---|
| Spring | Clean and repair | Remove old nests, check for damage, repair as needed |
| Spring | Install fresh nesting materials | Add soft materials for species like bluebirds |
| Summer | Monitor for activity | Watch for nesting birds and predators |
| Summer | Provide water sources | Ensure clean water is available nearby |
| Autumn | Post-nesting cleanup | Remove remaining nesting material |
| Autumn | Inspect for wear | Check for and repair any summer weather damage |
| Winter | Insulate if necessary | Add insulation for overwintering species in colder climates |
| Winter | Check mounting stability | Ensure birdhouses are secure against winter storms |

# Introduction to DIY Bird Feeders

Creating bird feeders from recycled materials is a fulfilling and eco-friendly activity. It provides a sustainable way to attract and support local bird populations and offers an excellent opportunity to repurpose items that might otherwise end up in landfills. This chapter will guide you through building and installing various bird feeders using common recycled materials.

## Benefits of Using Recycled Materials

- Environmental Impact: Reduces waste and promotes recycling.
- Cost-Effective: Lowers the cost of materials.
- Creativity: Encourages innovative designs using everyday items.
- Sustainability: Supports a circular economy and wildlife conservation.

**Types of Feeders: Platform, Tube, Hopper, and Suet Feeders**

Bird feeders come in several styles, each catering to different bird species and feeding habits.

- **Platform Feeders**: Simple and versatile, suitable for most birds.

Platform Feeder

- **Tube Feeders:** Cylindrical feeders are ideal for small birds like finches.
- **Hopper Feeders:** Gravity-fed feeders that store and dispense seeds as birds feed.
- **Suet Feeders:** Designed for holding suet cakes, attracting woodpeckers and other suet-eating birds.

Tube Feeder

Hopper Feeder

Suet Feeder

# Types of Feeders for Different Seed Preferences

## Overview of Bird Seed Types and Preferences

- **Sunflower Seeds**: Attracts various birds, including cardinals and chickadees.
- **Nyjer (Thistle) Seeds**: Preferred by finches and siskins.
- **Millet**: Attracts ground-feeding birds like sparrows and juncos.
- **Suet**: Appeals to woodpeckers, nuthatches, and wrens.

## Matching Feeders to Specific Bird Species

| FEEDER TYPE | SEED TYPE | TARGET BIRD SPECIES |
|---|---|---|
| Platform | Mixed Seed | Sparrows, Doves, Juncos |
| Tube | Nyjer (Thistle) | Finches, Pine Siskins |
| Hopper | Black Oil Sunflower | Cardinals, Blue Jays, Grosbeaks |
| Suet | Suet Cakes | Woodpeckers, Nuthatches, Wrens |

## Examples: Thistle Feeders for Finches, Suet Feeders for Woodpeckers

### Thistle Feeder for Finches

**Materials:** Old water bottle, wooden skewers.

**Steps:**
- Drill small holes around the bottle for feeding ports.
- Insert skewers as perches below each port.
- Fill with thistle seed and hang in a sheltered location.

**Suet Feeder for Woodpeckers**

**Materials:** Small log, wire mesh.

**Steps:**
- Hollow out part of the log to create a cavity.
- Fill the cavity with suet.
- Wrap wire mesh around the log to hold the suet in place.
- Attach hooks for hanging.

## Designing Seed Dispersal Mechanisms

### Gravity-Fed Systems

- Ensure even distribution by designing feeders with multiple small openings.
- Utilize gravity to keep seed flowing, refilling from a central storage area.

### Squirrel-Proofing Techniques

- Use baffles and cages to prevent squirrels from accessing the feeders.
- Place feeders on poles or hang them in locations difficult for squirrels to reach.

### Ensuring Even Seed Distribution

- Regularly check and clean feeders to prevent clogging.
- Design feeders with multiple ports and perches to accommodate more birds simultaneously.

Following these guidelines and plans, you can create functional and attractive bird feeders that enhance your backyard and support local wildlife. Enjoy the satisfaction of watching a variety of birds visit your handmade feeders!

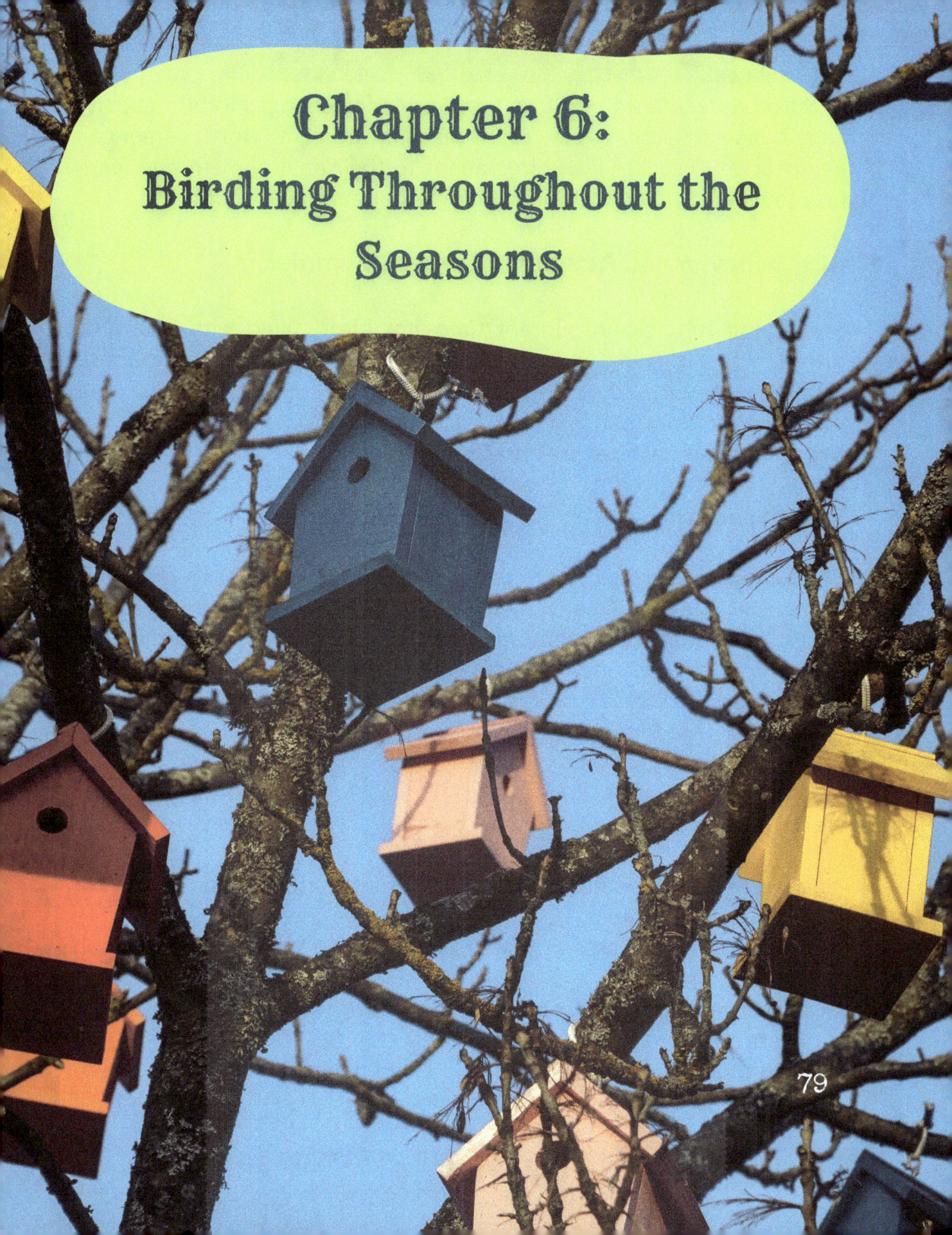

# Chapter 6: Birding Throughout the Seasons

In this chapter, we will explore the fascinating changes in bird activity and behavior across the four seasons from a North American perspective. Discover how birds adapt to their environment and learn how to enhance your backyard birding experience year-round.

## Bird Behavior and Activity in Spring & Summer

Spring and summer are vibrant times for birds, filled with courtship displays, nest building, and raising young. Let's delve deeper into these exciting events:

### Breeding Season: Nesting and Chick Rearing

**Spring Spectacle:**

- **Courtship Displays**: In North America, you can observe various species like the American Robin, Northern Cardinal, and Eastern Bluebird engaging in elaborate courtship displays to attract mates. Listen to their distinctive songs early in the morning.
- **Territorial Displays**: Birds like the Red-winged Blackbird and Northern Mockingbird establish and defend territories through song and physical displays.

**Nest Construction:**

**Nesting Styles:** Different birds use different materials and styles for their nests. For example:
- **Cavity Nesters:** Eastern Bluebirds and House Wrens use cavities in trees or birdhouses.
- **Platform Builders:** Ospreys and Mourning Doves build large, flat nests on platforms or tree branches.
- **Cup Nests:** American Robins and Goldfinches construct neat cup-shaped nests using grasses and mud.

**Cavity Nest**

**Platform Nest**

**Cup Nest**

## The Miracle of Life:

- **Clutch Size and Incubation:** Birds like the Tree Swallow typically lay 4-6 eggs, with an incubation period of around 14 days. Chickadees may lay up to 12 eggs with a similar incubation period.

- **Hatching and Fledging:** Observe the hatching process and fledgling behavior in species like the Northern Cardinal, where young birds leave the nest within 9-11 days after hatching.

## Watching Chicks Fledge:

- **Fledgling Behavior:** Look for young birds, such as fledgling robins, hopping around on the ground as they learn to fly. Provide a safe environment by keeping pets indoors and minimizing disturbances.

## Attracting Birds with Nesting Materials

### Nesting Needs:

- **Materials for Nests:** Different birds require different materials. For instance, Orioles use fibers and plant down, while Wrens prefer small twigs and feathers.

### Bird-Friendly Haven:

- **Natural Materials**: To help birds build their nests, place leaves, twigs, moss, and even pet hair in your yard. Ensure these materials are free of chemicals and pesticides.

### Alternative Nesting Options:

- **Birdhouses:** Install birdhouses suitable for local cavity nesters like the Eastern Bluebird or House Wren. Ensure proper dimensions and placement to attract these species.

## Recommended Birdhouse Specifications

| BIRD SPECIES | ENTRANCE HOLE DIAMETER | FLOOR DIMENSIONS (INCHES) | HEIGHT ABOVE GROUND (FEET) | NOTES |
|---|---|---|---|---|
| Eastern Bluebird | 1.5 inches | 5 x 5 | 4-6 | Place in open fields, spaced 100 feet apart |
| House Wren | 1 inch | 4 x 4 | 4-10 | Semi-shaded areas, near shrubs or small trees |
| American Kestrel | 3 inches | 8 x 8 | 10-30 | Open fields, clear line of sight |

## Fall Migration: Watching Birds on the Move

Fall brings a spectacular display of bird migration. Learn how to identify migratory patterns and enjoy the diverse feathered visitors:

### Migration Dynamics:

- Why Birds Migrate: Birds migrate to find food and suitable breeding grounds. For example, the Ruby-throated Hummingbird travels from North America to Central America to escape the cold and find nectar-rich flowers.

### Identifying Migrants:
- Common Migratory Species: Look for species like the Sandhill Crane, which migrates in large flocks, or the Warblers that pass through North American backyards in vibrant fall plumage.

## Creating a Stopover Haven:

- **Food and Shelter:** Provide high-energy foods like sunflower seeds and suet to support birds during their long journeys. Plant native shrubs and trees to offer natural shelter and food sources.

| BIRD SPECIES | PREFERRED FOOD | SHELTER | NOTES |
|---|---|---|---|
| Ruby-throated Hummingbird | Nectar, small insects | Dense shrubs, trees | Provide feeders with sugar water |
| Sandhill Crane | Grains, invertebrates | Wetlands, open fields | Large open spaces are essential |
| Warblers | Insects, berries | Dense foliage, mixed forests | Plant native berry-producing shrubs |

## Winter Birding: Providing Food and Shelter

As the weather turns cold, birds face new challenges. Learn how to support them and continue enjoying birdwatching throughout winter:

### Supplementing Natural Food Sources

**Birdseed Mixes:**
- **Seed Preferences:** Different species have different seed preferences. For instance, Black-capped Chickadees and Northern Cardinals favor black oil sunflower seeds, while American Goldfinches prefer nyjer (thistle) seeds.

## Setting Up Feeders:

- **Types of Feeders:** Use tube feeders for finches, platform feeders for sparrows, and suet feeders for woodpeckers.
- **Placement Strategies:** Place feeders in sheltered areas to protect birds from the wind. Ensure feeders are within view but safe from predators.

## Alternative Food Options:

- **Suet Cakes:** Offer high-energy suet cakes, especially appreciated by woodpeckers, nuthatches, and chickadees.
- **Fruits:** Provide fresh fruits like apples and oranges to attract species such as the American Robin and Cedar Waxwing.

## Winter Bird Food Preferences

| BIRD SPECIES | PREFERRED FOOD | FEEDER TYPE | NOTES |
|---|---|---|---|
| Black-capped Chickadee | Black oil sunflower seeds | Tube feeder | Place near trees for quick escape |
| Northern Cardinal | Black oil sunflower seeds | Platform feeder | Place in sheltered areas, near shrubs |
| American Goldfinch | Nyjer seeds | Tube feeder (small holes) | Keep feeders clean and dry |
| Downy Woodpecker | Suet | Suet feeder | Hang on tree trunks or sturdy branches |

## Keeping Water Sources Ice-Free

### Winter Hydration:

- **Importance of Water:** Birds need a reliable water source for drinking and bathing, even in winter.

### Heated Birdbaths:

- **Types of Heated Birdbaths:** Choose from immersion heaters, built-in heated birdbaths, or solar-heated options.
- **Considerations**: Ensure the birdbath is shallow with a rough surface for birds to grip.

### DIY Solutions:

- **Simple Methods**: Use black plastic dishes to absorb heat or place a small floating object to prevent complete freezing. Regularly replace the water to keep it fresh.

## Seasonal Birding Activities

| SEASON | KEY ACTIVITIES |
|---|---|
| Spring | Early morning songs, nest building, chick rearing |
| Summer | Fledgling observation, providing nesting materials |
| Fall | Identifying migratory patterns, creating stopover havens |
| Winter | Setting up feeders, keeping water sources ice-free |

By understanding and adapting to the seasonal behaviors and needs of birds, you can create a welcoming and supportive environment for various species throughout the year. Enjoy the dynamic and rewarding experience of backyard birdwatching in all seasons.

Bird Bath

# Chapter 7: Size, Shape, and Color as Birding Tools

Understanding the basics of bird identification is essential for novice and experienced birdwatchers. In this chapter, we'll explore how size, shape, and color can be powerful tools for identifying and appreciating the diverse bird species in North America.

## Understanding Bird Size

Bird size is one of the first clues in identifying a species. By comparing the size of an unknown bird to familiar birds, you can narrow down the possibilities. You can estimate the size of an unknown bird by comparing it to familiar birds like sparrows, robins, and crows. This initial comparison can quickly eliminate many possibilities. When you see a group of birds with different species, use the ones you already recognize to gauge the size of the unfamiliar bird. Measure essential body parts concerning the bird, such as bill length compared to the head, to aid identification.

### Relative Size Comparison

**Using Common Birds for Scale**

- Compare unknown birds to familiar species like robins, sparrows, or crows.
- Example: "The unknown bird was slightly larger than a sparrow but smaller than a robin."

| FAMILIAR BIRD | SIZE (INCHES) | SIZE (CENTIMETERS) | NOTES |
| --- | --- | --- | --- |
| House Sparrow | 6.3 | 16 | Small, common urban bird. |
| American Robin | 9.8 | 25 | Medium-sized, common in gardens. |
| American Crow | 17.5 | 45 | Large, commonly found in cities. |

## Size Categories

**Small Birds (Sparrow-sized and smaller):**

- Examples: Chickadees, warblers, and hummingbirds.
- Size range: 3-6 inches (8-15 cm).

Carolina chickadee

Warbler

**Medium Birds (Robin to crow-sized):**

- Examples: Jays, woodpeckers, and doves.
- Size range: 7-16 inches (18-41 cm).

Blue jay

Woodpecker

## Large Birds (Crow-sized and larger):

- Examples: Hawks, eagles, and herons.
- Size range: 17 inches and up (43 cm+).

Hawk

Eagle

| CATEGORY | EXAMPLE SPECIES | SIZE (INCHES) | SIZE (CENTIMETERS) | NOTES |
|---|---|---|---|---|
| Small Birds | Black-capped Chickadee | 5 | 13 | Common in forests and backyard feeders. |
| Medium Birds | Northern Flicker | 12.5 | 32 | Woodpecker often seen on the ground. |
| Large Birds | Great Blue Heron | 38-54 | 97-137 | Frequently found in wetlands and along shorelines. |

## Practical Examples

- House Sparrow vs. American Robin: Recognizing the size difference and using it as a critical identification tool.

- Red-tailed Hawk vs. Bald Eagle: Understanding how size can distinguish between large raptors.

## Analyzing Bird Shape

The shape of a bird provides additional clues, often linked to its behavior and habitat. This involves examining overall body structure, beak type, wing shape, and tail design.

## Body Structure

- **General Body Shape:**
    - Differences between plump, slender, or elongated bodies.
    - Example: A finch has a plump body compared to the slender body of a warbler.

- **Head Shape and Size:**
    - Variations in head proportions, crests, and facial features.
    - Example: A Northern Cardinal has a distinct crest compared to the smooth head of a Blue Jay.

## Beak Types

**Seed Eaters:**

- Short, stout beaks for cracking seeds.
- Examples: Finches and sparrows.

- **Insect Eaters:**
    - Thin, pointed beaks for catching insects.
    - Examples: Warblers and flycatchers.

- **Fish Eaters:**
    - Long, sharp beaks for catching fish.
    - Examples: Herons and kingfishers.

| BEAK TYPE | EXAMPLE SPECIES | NOTES |
|---|---|---|
| Short, Stout | House Finch | Uses beak to crack open seeds. |
| Thin, Pointed | Eastern Phoebe | Catches insects in flight. |
| Long, Sharp | Great Egret | Spears fish with its beak while wading in water. |

## Wing and Tail Shape

**Wing Shape:**

- Differences between broad, rounded raptors' wings and the swallows' pointed wings.

**Tail Shape:**

- Identifying forked, rounded, or square tails and their significance.
- Example: Swallows have a distinct forked tail compared to the rounded tail of a hawk.

| WING SHAPE | EXAMPLE SPECIES | NOTES |
|---|---|---|
| Broad, Rounded | Red-tailed Hawk | Soars on thermals with minimal flapping. |
| Pointed | Barn Swallow | Fast, agile flier catching insects in mid-air. |

## Practical Examples

- **Woodpecker's Sturdy Build**: Adaptations for pecking wood.
- **Swallow's Streamlined Shape**: Adaptations for swift aerial hunting.

## Deciphering Bird Color and Patterns

Coloration and patterning are often the most striking features and can provide definitive identification clues.

### Understanding Basic Color Terminology

- **Common Bird Colors:**

    - Recognizing primary colors like red, blue, and yellow and their variations.
    - Example: The bright blue of a Blue Jay vs. the deep red of a Northern Cardinal.

- **Iridescence and Gloss:**

    - Identifying birds with iridescent feathers like grackles and hummingbirds.

## Patterns and Markings

- **Stripes and Bars:**
    - Recognizing wing bars, tail bands, and streaks on the body.
    - Example: The wing bars on a Black-capped Chickadee.

- **Eye Rings and Wing Patches:**
    - Identifying birds by unique facial markings and wing spots.
    - Example: The distinctive eye ring of a Ruby-crowned Kinglet.

## Seasonal and Age-Related Changes

- **Breeding vs. Non-breeding Plumage:**
    - How colors can change with seasons, such as in warblers and buntings.
    - Example: American Goldfinch's bright yellow breeding plumage vs. olive winter plumage.

- **Juvenile vs. Adult Plumage:**
    - Identifying immature birds, which often have different colorings than adults.
    - Example: Juvenile Bald Eagles have mottled brown plumage compared to adults' iconic white heads.

| SPECIES | BREEDING PLUMAGE | NON-BREEDING PLUMAGE | JUVENILE PLUMAGE |
|---|---|---|---|
| American Goldfinch | Bright yellow | Olive green | Similar to non-breeding male |
| Northern Cardinal | Bright red (male) | Brownish-red (female) | Dull brown with hint of red |
| Eastern Bluebird | Bright blue and orange | Duller blue and gray | Grayish with faint blue |

## Practical Examples

- Northern Cardinal: Male's bright red plumage vs. female's muted tones.
- American Goldfinch: Bright yellow breeding plumage vs. olive winter plumage.

## Combining Size, Shape, and Color for Identification

Integrating all three elements provides a comprehensive approach to bird identification.

## Field Guides and Apps

- **Using Field Guides:**
    - How to utilize illustrations and descriptions effectively.
    - Example: Sibley Guide to Birds or Peterson Field Guide.

- **Bird Identification Apps:**
    - Leveraging technology like Merlin Bird ID or eBird for quick identification.

## Birding by Habitat

- **Linking Characteristics to Environment:**
    - Understanding how habitat influences bird size, shape, and color.
    - Example: Shorebirds in coastal areas vs. warblers in forests.

- **Examples of Habitat-Specific Birds:**
    - Shorebirds: Sandpipers, plovers.
    - Forest Birds: Woodpeckers, thrushes.
    - Grassland Species: Meadowlarks, sparrows.

## Practical Identification Exercises

- **Field Observation Techniques:**
    - Tips for noting and recording observations.
    - Example: Using a notebook or birding app to log sightings.

- **Creating a Bird Journal:**
    - Documenting sightings with sketches and notes on size, shape, and color.
    - Example: Drawing a robin and noting its size, rounded body, and red breast.

| OBSERVATION DATE | LOCATION | SPECIES | SIZE | SHAPE | COLOR AND PATTERNS | NOTES |
|---|---|---|---|---|---|---|
| 2024-05-18 | Central Park | American Robin | 9.8 inches | Rounded body, medium | Bright red breast, gray back, yellow beak | Seen foraging on the ground |
| 2024-05-20 | Local Wetland | Great Blue Heron | 38 inches | Long legs and neck | Gray-blue body, black stripe over eye | Observed wading in shallow water |
| 2024-05-22 | Backyard Feeder | Northern Cardinal | 8.3 inches | Plump body, crest | Bright red plumage (male), black mask around beak | Often visits feeder in the morning |

## Summary and Practice

Summarize key points and give practice exercises to reinforce learning.

### Key Takeaways

- **Summary of Size, Shape, and Color Importance:**
-
    - Reinforcement of identification skills.
    - Emphasize the integrated approach to using size, shape, and color for accurate identification.

**Practice Exercises**

- **Field Practice Scenarios:**

  - Provide hypothetical scenarios and encourage readers to identify birds based on given descriptions.
  - Example: "A bird with a short, stout beak, yellow body, and black wings—identify the species."

- **Bird Watching Challenges:**

  - Suggest challenges such as identifying ten different bird species in their local area using size, shape, and color as the primary tools.
  - Example: "Record and identify five bird species you see in your local park this weekend."

By mastering the use of size, shape, and color in bird identification, you'll become a more skilled and confident birdwatcher, able to appreciate the incredible diversity of avian life in North America.

# Chapter 8:
# Beyond Your Backyard: Exploring Birding Locations

This chapter will explore birding hotspots across North America. Each region boasts unique habitats and bird species, offering endless opportunities for birdwatching adventures. Discover the best locations to observe and enjoy North America's diverse avian life, from national parks and wildlife refuges to urban oases and coastal regions.

## Finding Local Birding Hotspots

North America offers a wealth of birding locations, each with its unique bird species and habitats. This section will guide you through some prime birding hotspots you can explore.

### Wildlife Refuges and National Parks

| LOCATION | HABITAT | KEY SPECIES | BEST TIME TO VISIT |
|---|---|---|---|
| Yellowstone National Park (WY, MT, ID) | Mixed forests, meadows, geothermal areas | Bald Eagle, Trumpeter Swan, American Dipper | Spring/Summer (breeding), Fall (migration) |
| Everglades National Park (FL) | Wetlands, mangroves, sawgrass marshes | Roseate Spoonbill, Wood Stork, Snail Kite | Winter/Early Spring (highest diversity) |
| Chincoteague National Wildlife Refuge (VA) | Coastal marshes, beaches, maritime forests | Snow Goose, Piping Plover, American Oystercatcher | Fall/Winter (waterfowl), Spring (shorebirds) |
| Bosque del Apache National Wildlife Refuge (NM) | Wetlands, riparian areas, arid uplands | Sandhill Crane, Snow Goose, American Avocet | Late Fall/Winter (crane & goose migration) |

## State Parks and Local Forests

Often overlooked gems, state parks, and local forests can be havens for resident and migratory birds. Consider these examples:

| LOCATION | HABITAT | KEY SPECIES | BEST TIME TO VISIT |
|---|---|---|---|
| High Island (TX) | Coastal woodlands, salt marshes | Migratory songbirds, Reddish Egret, Clapper Rail | Spring & Fall (migration) |
| Adirondack Park (NY) | Boreal forests, lakes, wetlands | Common Loon, Black-backed Woodpecker, Boreal Chickadee | Summer (breeding), Fall (foliage & birding) |
| Redwood National and State Parks (CA) | Coastal redwoods, rivers, prairies | Marbled Murrelet, Northern Spotted Owl, American Dipper | Spring/Summer (breeding, mild weather) |

## Coastal Areas and Wetlands

These dynamic ecosystems provide vital stopovers and breeding grounds for many bird species. Here are some captivating locations:

| LOCATION | HABITAT | KEY SPECIES | BEST TIME TO VISIT |
|---|---|---|---|
| Cape May (NJ) | Beaches, salt marshes, forests | Red Knot, Black Skimmer, Peregrine Falcon | Fall (raptor migration), Spring (shorebirds & songbirds) |
| Point Reyes National Seashore (CA) | Coastal scrub, grasslands, forests | Western Gull, Pigeon Guillemot, White-crowned Sparrow | Year-round (peak in spring & fall) |
| Everglades National Park (FL) | Included for completeness (see Wildlife Refuges) | Roseate Spoonbill, Wood Stork, Snail Kite | Winter/Early Spring (highest diversity) |

## Urban Birding Oases

Even within bustling cities, green spaces can offer surprising birding opportunities. Here are some examples:

| LOCATION | HABITAT | KEY SPECIES | BEST TIME TO VISIT |
|---|---|---|---|
| Central Park (New York City, NY) | Urban park with woodlands, meadows, water bodies | Warblers, Red-tailed Hawk, Eastern Screech-Owl | Spring & Fall (migration) |
| Golden Gate Park (San Francisco, CA) | Urban park with forests, lakes, and gardens | Anna's Hummingbird, Western Bluebird, Great Horned Owl | Year-round (diverse species throughout seasons) |
| Mont-Royal Park (Montreal, Quebec) | Urban park with mixed woodlands and meadows | American Redstart, Black-capped Chickadee, Cooper's Hawk | Spring & Fall (migration) |

## Nationwide Surveys

These large-scale projects provide valuable snapshots of bird populations across North America.

- **Great Backyard Bird Count (GBBC)**: An annual event (usually in February) where participants of all ages count birds in their backyards or local areas. Submit your data online to contribute to a real-time snapshot of winter bird distribution.

- **Christmas Bird Count (CBC)**: The longest-running citizen science survey in the world (since 1900). Volunteers conduct intensive bird counts over 24 hours in designated areas around Christmas. Joining a local CBC circle allows you to contribute to this crucial dataset.

## Regional Monitoring Programs

These ongoing programs track bird populations in specific regions or habitats.

- **eBird**: A free online platform (website and app) where birdwatchers can record their sightings throughout the year. This real-time data contributes to a massive global database for scientific research, conservation efforts, and bird identification.
- **NestWatch**: A nationwide program that monitors the nesting success of birds. Volunteers monitor bird nests in their area, recording data on breeding activity, hatching rates, and fledgling survival.

Additional Citizen Science Opportunities: Many regional bird observatories, local Audubon chapters, and conservation organizations offer citizen science projects focused on specific bird species or habitats. Research opportunities in your area to find a project that aligns with your interests.

## Joining Birding Clubs and Online Communities

**Local Birding Clubs**

Bird clubs offer a welcoming environment to:
- Find Local Clubs: Search online directories of birding organizations like the National Audubon Society or enquire at local nature centers or bird observatories.
- Join a Local Chapter: Participate in organized field trips to birding hotspots led by experienced birders.
- Expand Your Knowledge: Attend workshops and talks on bird identification, birding ethics, and habitat conservation.
- Network with Fellow Birders: Connect with other birders to share sightings, learn identification tips, and build lasting friendships.

## Online Birding Forums and Social Media Groups

The online birding community offers a wealth of information and opportunities to connect:

- Birding Forums: Websites like BirdForum.net or online forums hosted by birdwatching magazines provide platforms for discussing bird sightings, identification challenges, and birding experiences.
- Social Media Groups: Join Facebook groups dedicated to birding in your region or focused on specific bird groups (like raptors or warblers). Share your sightings, get help with bird identification, and be inspired by other birders' experiences.
- Follow Hashtags: Follow hashtags like #birding and #birdwatching on Instagram or Twitter to discover stunning bird photos, learn about new birding locations, and engage with the broader birding community.

By actively participating in online communities, you can:

- Stay updated on local bird sightings and birding events.
- Learn from experienced birders and hone your identification skills.
- Share your birding experiences and inspire others.

## Creating Your Birding Logbook

Keeping a detailed birding logbook is essential for tracking your sightings, improving your birding skills, and reminiscing about your birding adventures.

## Logbook Essentials

Record the following information for each bird sighting:

- Date and Time: Note the date and time of your observation.
- Location: Include the specific location (park name, trail, etc.) and consider adding GPS coordinates for future reference.
- Weather Conditions: Briefly describe the weather conditions (sunny, cloudy, windy) as weather can influence bird behavior.
- Species Observed: List the bird species you observed, using common names and scientific names if known.
- Number of Individuals: Record the number of birds you saw for each species.
- Behavior Notes: Describe the bird's behavior (feeding, calling, flying patterns)

## Sample Logbook Entry:

| DATE | LOCATION | SPECIES | NUMBER | BEHAVIOR NOTES | WEATHER |
|---|---|---|---|---|---|
| 2024-05-25 | Golden Gate Park, CA | Anna's Hummingbird | 2 | Hovering near red flowers | Sunny, 72°F |

Additional Tips:

- Use a notebook that is easy to carry in the field.
- Consider using waterproof paper or a laminated cover to protect your notes from the elements.

# Conclusion

Backyard Birds: A Beginner Birdwatching Guide has taken you through the captivating world of birdwatching, from your backyard to the diverse landscapes of North America. Here's a brief recap of what we've covered:

- **Attracting Birds**: Learn how to make your backyard a haven for birds by providing food, water, shelter, and nesting sites tailored to different species.

- **Identifying Birds**: Master bird identification through size, shape, and color, enhancing your appreciation of their beauty and behavior.

- **Photographing Birds**: Improve your bird photography skills to create stunning visual records of your observations.

- **Bird Identification Records**: Keep detailed logs of your sightings to track bird diversity and habits over time.

- **DIY Projects**: Build birdhouses, feeders, and custom seed mixes with beginner-friendly projects that benefit local birds.

- **Exploring Beyond Your Backyard**: Discover local birding hotspots, participate in citizen science projects, and enjoy rich birding experiences in national parks, wildlife refuges, and urban areas.

**The Joy of Birdwatching:** Birdwatching is a lifelong hobby filled with endless discovery and connection with nature. Whether you're a casual observer or a dedicated birder, the joy lies in observing and appreciating the avian world.

**Your Role in Conservation:**

By creating bird-friendly environments and engaging in citizen science, you contribute valuable data to bird conservation efforts, ensuring future generations can enjoy these avian wonders.

**Looking Ahead:**
Explore new birding locations, engage with communities, and expand your knowledge. Birds are remarkable creatures; the more you learn, the deeper your appreciation will become.

Thank you for joining Backyard Birds: A Beginner Birdwatching Guide. May your days be filled with birds' delightful sights and sounds, and may your backyard be a sanctuary where they thrive and inspire.

**Happy Birdwatching!**

Please let us know how we're doing by leaving us a review.

# Chapter 9: Appendix

# APPENDIX 1 - GLOSSARY

## Birding Lingo: A Glossary for Beginning Birdwatchers

- Birdwatching may seem simple, but it has its lingo and terminology. Here's a helpful glossary to get you started:
- General Birding Terms:
- BINS (or Binoculars): Essential tool for magnified views of birds.
- Birder: Someone interested in watching and studying birds (more dedicated than a casual "birdwatcher").
- Birding: The activity of watching and studying birds in their natural habitat.
- Bogey Bird: A bird you see but can't quite identify, often leaving you frustrated.
- CBC (Christmas Bird Count): The longest-running citizen science survey, where volunteers count birds over 24 hours in December.
- Dip: Missing a bird you hoped to see at a birding location.
- Flight: The manner a bird flies is helpful for identification (e.g., undulating, direct).
- Flock: A group of birds of the same or similar species flying or feeding together.
- Habitat: The natural environment where a particular bird species lives.
- LBJ (Little Brown Job): A humorous term for a small, brown bird that's difficult to identify to species.
- Life List: A personal record of all the bird species a birder has seen.
- Lifer: A new bird species added to your life list.
- Plumage: A bird's feathers and their color patterns.
- Preening: A bird cleaning and arranging its feathers with its beak.
- Song: A complex vocalization used by male birds to attract mates and defend territories.
- Territorial: Behavior where a bird defends a specific area from other birds of the same species.
- Twitch (or Twitching): Traveling specifically to see a rare bird species.
- Wader/Shorebird: Birds that live near water margins and have long legs for wading.

# APPENDIX 1 - GLOSSARY

## Birding Lingo: A Glossary for Beginning Birdwatchers

- Bird Size and Shape:
- Mantle: The upper back of a bird, between the wings.
- Rump: The area at the base of the tail.
- Underparts: The underside of a bird, including the breast, belly, and undertail coverts.
- Wingbar: A contrasting patch of color on a bird's wing.
- Bird Behavior:
- Call: A simpler vocalization than a song, used for communication between birds.
- Foraging: A bird searching for food.
- Molt: The process of losing and replacing old feathers with new ones.
- Perching: A bird resting on a branch or other object.
- Soaring: A bird gliding on air currents without flapping its wings.
- Citizen Science:
- eBird: A free online platform to record bird sightings and contribute to a global database.
- Additional Terms:
- Birding by Ear: Identifying birds based on their vocalizations.
- Ethical Birding: Minimizing disturbance to birds and their habitat.
- Patch: A favorite birding location, often close to home.
- Scope (or Spotting Scope): A high-powered telescope for distant birdwatching.
- Slough: A marshy area with soft, wet ground.
- Snag: A dead or dying standing tree, critical habitat for some bird species.
- By understanding this essential birding glossary, you'll be better equipped to communicate with other birders, understand field guides, and enhance your birding adventures!

# APPENDIX 2

# Bird Seed Mix Recipes for Different Seasons

Here's a table outlining potential bird seed mixes for different seasons, considering the birds' natural dietary changes:

| SEASON | BIRD SEED MIX | KEY INGREDIENTS | WHY |
|---|---|---|---|
| Spring & Summer (Breeding Season) | Energy Boost | * Black Oil Sunflower Seeds (high in fat) * Nyjer Seeds (thistle) * Dried Mealworms * Suet Pellets | Provides extra energy for nesting, chick rearing, and increased activity. |
| Fall (Migration & Prepping for Winter) | High-Calorie Mix | * Hulled Sunflower Seeds * Cracked Corn * Peanuts * Mixed Shelled Nuts | Offers rich calories for building fat reserves for migration and harsh winter conditions. |
| Winter (Cold Weather) | Suet & Nutty Mix | * Suet Cakes * Suet Dough * Shelled Peanuts * Mixed Tree Seeds | Provides high-fat suet for warmth and energy, along with nuts and seeds for essential nutrients. |

## Additional Notes:

- This is a general guideline, and you can adjust the ingredients based on your local bird species and their preferences.
- Always offer fresh water alongside your birdseed mix.
- Avoid using millet or milo fillers, as many birds discard them.
- Add sliced fruit (apples, oranges) in warmer months for additional moisture and a sweet treat.
- Research native plants that produce seeds and berries. Plant them in your yard to provide a natural food source for birds.

# APPENDIX 3
## Free Online Bird Identification Resources

Identifying birds can be a fun and rewarding challenge. Here are some excellent free online resources to help you on your birding journey:

## 1. Cornell Lab of Ornithology - All About Birds:

*https://www.allaboutbirds.org/news/*

- This is a general guideline, and you can adjust the ingredients based on your local bird species and their preferences.
- Always offer fresh water alongside your birdseed mix.
- Avoid using millet or milo fillers, as many birds discard them.
- Add sliced fruit (apples, oranges) in warmer months for additional moisture and a sweet treat.
- Research native plants that produce seeds and berries. Plant them in your yard to provide birds with a natural food source.
- Features:
- Extensive species profiles with detailed descriptions, range maps, photos, and audio recordings of bird calls and songs.
- Beginner's guides on bird identification basics (size, shape, behavior, habitat).
- Interactive quizzes and games to test your bird identification skills.

## 2. The Merlin Bird ID App by Cornell Lab of Ornithology:

- Platform: Free app available for iOS and Android devices.
- Features:
    - Answer a series of questions about the bird you saw (size, color, behavior, location).
    - Merlin uses your answers and real-time data to suggest a shortlist of most likely bird species.
    - Each species entry includes photos, range maps, and audio recordings.

# APPENDIX 3
## Free Online Bird Identification Resources

**3. eBird:**
Website: *https://ebird.org/home*
**Features**:
- Interactive online checklist for recording your bird sightings and contributing to a global birding database.
- You can explore sightings from your area or anywhere worldwide to see what other birders are finding.
- The "Explore" function filters sightings by location, date, and species.
- Photo galleries with user-submitted images of birds from all over the world.

**4. National Audubon Society:**

Website: *https://www.audubon.org/*

- Features:
  - Field guides with photos and descriptions of North American bird species.
  - Interactive quizzes and games to test your bird identification skills.
  - Local chapters and birding resources across North America.

**5. The Macaulay Library at the Cornell Lab of Ornithology:**

- Website: *https://www.macaulaylibrary.org/*

- Features:
  - Massive archive of free, high-quality bird sounds, photos, and videos.
  - Search by species name, location, habitat, or behavior.
  - A great resource for learning bird songs and calls.

# APPENDIX 4

# Seasonal Bird Migration Charts

## Spring Migration Patterns and Peak Times

| SPECIES | STARTING REGION | DESTINATION REGION | PEAK MIGRATION PERIOD | KEY STOPOVER SITES |
|---|---|---|---|---|
| Ruby-throated Hummingbird | Central America | Eastern North America | Late March – Early May | Gulf Coast, Great Lakes |
| Sandhill Crane | Southern U.S., Mexico | Northern U.S., Canada | March – April | Platte River, Nebraska; Monte Vista NWR |
| Blackpoll Warbler | South America | Eastern Canada, New England | May | Gulf Coast, Appalachian Mountains |
| American Robin | Southern U.S., Mexico | Northern U.S., Canada | March – April | Throughout U.S., particularly forests and suburbs |

## Fall Migration Patterns and Peak Times

| SPECIES | STARTING REGION | DESTINATION REGION | PEAK MIGRATION PERIOD | KEY STOPOVER SITES |
|---|---|---|---|---|
| Arctic Tern | Arctic regions | Antarctic regions | September – October | Coastal areas of North America |
| Yellow Warbler | Northern U.S., Canada | Central and South America | August – September | Coastal and inland riparian zones |
| Broad-winged Hawk | Eastern North America | Central and South America | September | Hawk Mountain, Pennsylvania; Veracruz, Mexico |
| Swainson's Thrush | Northern U.S., Canada | Central and South America | September – October | Along the Rocky Mountains, Central U.S. |

# APPENDIX 4

## Key Migration Corridors in North America

| MIGRATION CORRIDOR | DESCRIPTION | MAJOR SPECIES | PEAK MIGRATION PERIOD |
|---|---|---|---|
| Atlantic Flyway | Follows the Atlantic Coast from the Arctic to the tropics | Shorebirds, Warblers, Raptors | Spring: March – May; Fall: August – October |
| Mississippi Flyway | Follows the Mississippi River through the central U.S. | Ducks, Geese, Sandhill Cranes, Songbirds | Spring: March – May; Fall: August – October |
| Central Flyway | Runs through the Great Plains from Canada to Central America | Waterfowl, Hawks, Sandhill Cranes | Spring: March – May; Fall: August – October |
| Pacific Flyway | Follows the Pacific Coast from Alaska to South America | Seabirds, Waterfowl, Raptors | Spring: March – May; Fall: August – October |

## Sample Birdwatching Logbook Entry for Migratory Birds

| DATE | SPECIES | LOCATION | BEHAVIOR OBSERVED | WEATHER CONDITIONS | NOTES |
|---|---|---|---|---|---|
| 04/15/2024 | Ruby-throated Hummingbird | Gulf Coast, Texas | Feeding on nectar, hovering | Sunny, 75°F | First sighting of the season, observed feeding at red tubular flowers |
| 09/20/2024 | Broad-winged Hawk | Hawk Mountain, PA | Soaring in large kettles | Clear, 68°F | Counted over 500 hawks in one day, part of the peak migration period |
| 10/05/2024 | Swainson's Thrush | Rocky Mountains, CO | Foraging in berry bushes | Partly cloudy, 60°F | Observed multiple individuals in the area, fattening up for the journey ahead |

# APPENDIX 5
# Bird Photography Tips

Capturing stunning photographs of birds requires a mix of patience, technique, and the right equipment. This appendix offers practical advice on camera settings, composition tips, and techniques tailored to various environments and bird behaviors to help you enhance your bird photography skills.

## Camera Settings for Bird Photography

1. **Shutter Speed:**
   - Fast-moving birds (e.g., in-flight): 1/1000 sec or faster.
   - Perched or slow-moving birds: 1/250 - 1/500 sec.
2. **Aperture:**
   - Shallow depth of field (isolating the bird): f/4 to f/6.3.
   - Greater depth of field (including more of the environment): f/8 to f/11.
3. **ISO:**
   - Good lighting conditions: ISO 100 - 400.
   - Low light or overcast conditions: ISO 800 - 1600 (higher ISO may introduce noise).
4. **Focus Mode:**
   - Single Point AF: For precise focus on the bird's eye.
   - Continuous AF: For tracking birds in motion.
5. **Drive Mode:**
   - Continuous Shooting: Allows multiple shots quickly to capture the perfect moment.

## Composition Tips

- **Rule of Thirds**: Position the bird off-center to create a more dynamic and engaging image.
- **Leading Lines**: Use natural elements like branches or water lines to lead the viewer's eye towards the bird.
- **Background:** To make the bird stand out, opt for clean, non-distracting backgrounds. Use a wide aperture to blur the background (bokeh effect).

# APPENDIX 5

## Camera Settings for Bird Photography

1. **Shutter Speed:**
   - Fast-moving birds (e.g., in-flight): 1/1000 sec or faster.
   - Perched or slow-moving birds: 1/250 - 1/500 sec.
2. **Aperture:**
   - Shallow depth of field (isolating the bird): f/4 to f/6.3.
   - Greater depth of field (including more of the environment): f/8 to f/11.
3. **ISO:**
   - Good lighting conditions: ISO 100 - 400.
   - Low light or overcast conditions: ISO 800 - 1600 (higher ISO may introduce noise).
4. **Focus Mode:**
   - Single Point AF: For precise focus on the bird's eye.
   - Continuous AF: For tracking birds in motion.
5. **Drive Mode:**
   - Continuous Shooting: Allows multiple shots quickly to capture the perfect moment.

## Composition Tips

- **Rule of Thirds**: Position the bird off-center to create a more dynamic and engaging image.
- **Leading Lines**: Use natural elements like branches or water lines to lead the viewer's eye towards the bird.
- **Background:** To make the bird stand out, opt for clean, non-distracting backgrounds. Use a wide aperture to blur the background (bokeh effect).

# APPENDIX 5

**Framing:**
- Use natural frames such as foliage, tree branches, or other elements to add depth and focus to the image.

**Behavioral Shots:**
- Capture birds engaging in natural behaviors such as feeding, nesting, or preening to add interest and context to your photos.

Techniques for Different Environments and Behaviors

1. **Forest and Woodland Birds:**
   - **Techniques:** Use higher ISO settings to compensate for low light under the canopy. Focus on the eyes and ensure a shutter speed that is fast enough to avoid motion blur.
   - **Examples:** Woodpeckers, warblers, and owls.
2. **Wetlands and Water Birds:**
   - **Techniques:** Use a tripod for stability when photographing from a distance. Early morning or late afternoon light often provides the best conditions.
   - **Examples:** Herons, ducks, and egrets.
3. **Open Fields and Grasslands:**
   - **Techniques:** Use long telephoto lenses to capture birds from a distance without disturbing them. Monitor wind direction to ensure the light is on the bird's face.
   - **Examples:** Hawks, larks, and sparrows.
4. **Coastal and Shorebirds:**
   - **Techniques:** Timing is key; shoot during low tide when birds are foraging. Use a low angle to create a more intimate perspective.
   - **Examples:** Sandpipers, gulls, and plovers.
5. **Urban and Suburban Birds:**
   - **Techniques:** Focus on areas where birds congregate, such as parks, gardens, and feeders. Urban backgrounds can add unique context to your shots.
   - **Examples:** Pigeons, sparrows, and finches.

# APPENDIX 5

## Sample Bird Photography Logbook Entry

| DATE | SPECIES | LOCATION | CAMERA SETTINGS | BEHAVIOR OBSERVED | NOTES |
|---|---|---|---|---|---|
| 05/10/2024 | American Goldfinch | Backyard feeder | 1/500 sec, f/5.6, ISO 400, Single Point AF | Feeding on sunflower seeds | Captured several shots of feeding behavior, best light was in the early morning |
| 08/15/2024 | Great Blue Heron | Local wetland | 1/1000 sec, f/8, ISO 800, Continuous AF | Fishing in shallow water | Early morning shoot, used a tripod for stability, great reflections on water |
| 10/05/2024 | Peregrine Falcon | Coastal cliff | 1/2000 sec, f/6.3, ISO 1600, Continuous Shooting | In-flight hunting dive | High shutter speed essential for sharp action shots, overcast lighting helped reduce shadows |

## We'd Love Your Feedback!

Please let us know how we're doing by leaving us a review.

# APPENDIX 6

# Birdwatching Logbook Page

**OBSERVER INFORMATION**

Name: _____

Date: _____

Location: _____

Weather Conditions: _____

**BIRD SIGHTING DETAILS**

| SPECIES | NUMBER OF INDIVIDUALS | TIME | HABITAT | BEHAVIOR OBSERVED | ADDITIONAL NOTES |
|---|---|---|---|---|---|
|  |  |  |  |  |  |
|  |  |  |  |  |  |
|  |  |  |  |  |  |

**ADDITIONAL OBSERVATIONS AND NOTES**

Notes

_____

_____

_____

# Birdwatching Logbook Page

**SKETCHES OR PHOTOS**

- Sketches or Photos
  ------------------------------------------------

- Description of Sketch
  ------------------------------------------------

- PhotoAttached(Y/N)
  ------------------------------------------------

**SUMMARY OF DAY'S OBSERVATIONS**

| | |
|---|---|
| Total Species Observed | ------------------------ |
| Most Interesting Sighting | ------------------------ |
| Any Rare or Unusual Sightings | ------------------------ |
| Overall Experience | ------------------------ |

**BIRDWATCHING TIPS AND LEARNINGS**

Tips and Learnings
------------------------------------------------
------------------------------------------------
------------------------------------------------

www.ingramcontent.com/pod-product-compliance
Lightning Source LLC
Chambersburg PA
CBHW080215040426
42333CB00044B/2679